Inequality in American Society

**Scott, Foresman Series in
Institutions and Modern Social Problems**

Gresham M. Sykes, Editor

Core Volume

SOCIAL PROBLEMS IN AMERICA, Gresham M. Sykes

Auxiliary volumes cover the following topics:

COMMUNITY, William Simon

FAMILY

POLITICS

INEQUALITY, Leonard Reissman

WORK, Seymour Wolfbein

EDUCATION, David Gottlieb

VALUES

Inequality in American Society

SOCIAL STRATIFICATION

Leonard Reissman
Cornell University

Scott, Foresman and Company

GLENVIEW, ILLINOIS   BRIGHTON, ENGLAND

Cover Photo: Françoise Nicolas

Library of Congress Catalog Card Number: 72–91698
ISBN: 0–673–05921–9

Regional offices of Scott, Foresman and Company
are located in Dallas, Texas; Glenview, Illinois;
Oakland, New Jersey; Palo Alto, California;
Tucker, Georgia; and Brighton, England.

To
Ethel
For Everything

Acknowledgements

From "Poverty As Income Deficiency: Three Approaches" from *The Future of Inequality* by S. M. Miller and Pamela A. Roby. Reprinted by permission of Basic Books, Inc., Publishers.

From "Poverty: Changing Social Stratification" from *The Future of Inequality* by S. M. Miller and Pamela Roby. Reprinted by permission of Basic Books, Inc., Publishers.

From "Black Matriarchy Reconsidered" by Herbert H. Hyman and John Shelton Reed from *Public Opinion Quarterly*, 33 (Fall 1969). Reprinted by permission of *The Public Opinion Quarterly* and the authors.

From *Democracy in America* by Alexis de Tocqueville, translated by George Lawrence and edited by J. P. Mayer. Reprinted by permission of Harper & Row, Publishers, Inc. and Fontana Paperbacks.

From *Challenge to the Court: Social Scientists and the Defense of Segregation*, 1954–1966 by I. A. Newby. © 1967 by the Louisiana State University Press. Reprinted by permission of the publishers.

"The Black Establishment" by Colin Legum. This article first appeared in *New Society*, the weekly review of the social sciences, 128 Long Acre, London W C 2. Reprinted by permission.

From *Democracy in America* by Alexis de Tocqueville, translated by Henry Reeve and edited by Henry Steele Commager. © 1947 by the Oxford University Press. Reprinted by permission of the publisher.

Reprinted with permission from the *Proceedings of the Academy of Political Science*, 29 (July 1968).

From *The Impossible Revolution* by Lewis M. Killian. Reprinted by permission of Random House, Inc.

From "Readiness to Succeed: Mobility Aspirations and Modernism Among the Poor" by Leonard Reissman. Reprinted from *Urban Affairs Quarterly*, 4, No. 3 (March 1969): 379–98, by permission of the Publisher, Sage Publications, Inc.

From *Social Mobility in Industrial Society* by Seymour Martin Lipset and Reinhard Bendix, University of California Press, 1959. Originally published by the University of California Press; reprinted by permission of The Regents of the University of California.

From "Income and Stratification Ideology: Beliefs About the American Opportunity Structure" by Joan H. Rytina, William H. Form, and John Pease. Reprinted from the *American Journal of Sociology*, 75 (January 1970). Reprinted by permission of the University of Chicago Press.

From "Subjective Social Class in America: 1945–1968" by E. M. Schreiber and G. T. Nygreen. *Social Forces*, 48 (March 1970): 351. © by the University of North Carolina Press. Reprinted by permission of the publisher.

Foreword

The study of American social problems has grown too complex for any one person to feel comfortable in claiming expertise in all its parts. What is needed, we believe, is a twofold approach to this important area of sociology: a general overview that can tie the major social problems of our society together in a common conceptual framework and a series of books written by different authors analyzing each major social problem in depth. It is this cooperative effort that forms the Scott, Foresman Series in Institutions and Modern Social Problems.

The basic idea uniting this series of books is that social problems are best viewed as a discrepancy between ideals and reality, between a *vision* of what society should be like and the *reality* of our present social institutions. In the writings of a number of sociologists, the existing form of society is not regarded as posing difficulties. Rather, social problems are apt to be defined as a failure to adhere to the norms of the status quo or as a breakdown of the norms themselves. But these definitions give us few guidelines for separating serious and trivial issues: They assume too readily a normative consensus when there is actually a good deal of conflict, and they tend to overlook the extent to which existing social norms may be the most important problem of all.

Our definition of social problems—as the failure of existing social institutions to fulfill an ideal of a society—admittedly lacks a certain academic neatness, but we believe that it provides the basis for a legitimate and important field of study. This series reflects the idea that the problems encountered in one institutional area are linked to those found in another and that there are some common threads running through our present dilemmas. And if a comprehensive causal explanation is something of a chimera, it is still true that the social sciences can greatly aid our understanding of the forces at work in particular institutional areas and the possibilities for reform. We are beginning to learn about the factors influencing man's environment in cities and suburbs, the role of the family in socialization, the impact of educational systems, the meaning of work, social inequality, the exercise of power, and the role of ultimate values. It is, we think, at this relatively modest level of "theories of the middle range" that the social sciences can make a significant contribution to the solution of the social problems that plague us.

Leonard Reissman's book addresses itself to one of the fundamental ideals of American society—a belief in equality—and the reality we have created in the latter part of the twentieth century. Focusing mainly on the problems of racial minorities and the poor, Professor Reissman illuminates our ambivalent attitudes toward those at the bottom of the social heap, the distance we have come and the distance we still have to go in developing eqalitarianism, the varieties of inequality and their causes, and the possibilities that are now before us. *Inequality in American Society: Social Stratification* places the problem of who gets what in our society into a theoretical and historical perspective. It provides a firm awareness of what Gunnar Myrdal called our "national schizophrenia"—our willingness to pay lip service to equality without taking action. The author offers no simple remedy, pointing instead to the limits of both ideology and social engineering; but the forces that may build a more equal society are presented with realism and are elucidated in a style that is free from jargon.

Gresham M. Sykes,
Editor

Preface

It is within the American temperament to save our attention for issues that appear—or are made to appear—as critical or problematic. This trait necessarily forces a rhetoric of increasingly dramatic superlatives so as to command attention and move it from one issue to another. Like a hurricane that magnifies and increases over water, so too does this rhetoric push ever more dramatically in order to make the point against the background of existing dramatic and inflated rhetorics.

Such escalation very quickly hypnotizes our sensibilities and judgments. The calmer vocabulary has been made useless so that we become unable to make rational comparisons between competing issues over the full spectrum of possibilities. Every change tends to become phrased as revolutionary change; mere difficulties become vital problems; growth becomes a threatening explosion; and discussions become inflexible confrontations. Thereby, anything that is only slightly problematic (by any sane standard) is jumbled together with what is critical. The problem, for instance, of drug abuse is elevated in importance to the same level as, for example, racial violence; traffic congestion becomes just as important as housing congestion.

It is virtually impossible to sustain serious attention for very long at an unrelieved high pitch. As with children whose attention span is limited, adult Americans appear to cast about for ever-different social problems to occupy them. Recognizing this human limitation, political leaders have learned to spot new social issues which they can identify as their own and with which they can move into center stage for public attention. How else can we account for the succession of problems that have whirled past us during the past decade? From the problems of race and of poverty not so long ago, we have jumped to crime, drugs, women's liberation, and even more recently to the problems of population growth, pollution, and ecology. We are at a point where we are attacking the task of paper and bottle recycling with the same fervor that we expended not so long ago for the glaring problems inherent in poverty. Such fickleness and such uncritical allocation of human and social resources are hardly conducive to attracting and sustaining the serious attention that is required for seeking reasonable solutions.

The point of these comments is to win the reader's attention back to the problems associated with social inequality in American society. Although the American consciousness apparently has become jaded by these problems and although attention has been switched to other issues, inequality still remains truly critical for our society. The Mississippi summers, the war on poverty, black power, and other symbols of a once-intense concern with inequalities are behind us; they have been moved off the front pages and even downgraded in the federal budget. Nevertheless, the problems of inequality will not so easily fade; instead, they will keep on growing whether we recognize them or not.

Racial and economic inequalities, as they are analyzed in this book, will continue to generate some of the most serious problems for American society in the future, just as they have in the past. As I write, for example, school bussing has moved again to the forefront of our attention. Once again we are confronted as a society with the choice between a step toward racial integration in the public schools and a step backward to continued segregation—whatever noble rationale is offered in support. It is as if the Supreme Court's decision of 1954 had never been made. To take another instance, once again we are being told that people are on welfare because they are lazy and do not want to work for a living, as if the voluminous documentation over the past decade about the social causes of poverty had never been written. In short, the subject of inequality must persist, whether we like it or not, because it is interwoven into the fabric of American society.

The subject of this book, therefore, must not become outdated whatever the vagaries of public attention, pragmatic politics, or competing social issues. Although its particular manifestatiions will change, I am afraid that social inequalities are with us for some time to come. The reasons that support this conclusion are detailed in the pages that follow.

Another thread woven throughout this book that I wish to make explicit here, is that the suggested solutions for inequality—in the past and in the future—are intimately tied to the way in which the problems of inequality are defined. Instead of trying to argue for one solution or another, I have chosen deliberately to direct the discussion to the manner in which the problems of inequality are phrased. This is no idle exercise, for I am entirely convinced that problem definitions shape the social reality we perceive, and consequently, the solutions that are possible. To encourage an understanding and appreciation for this sequence is, in a real sense, a primary objective of this book.

Leonard Reissman

Contents

Inequality in American Society

1
Equality As a Positive Goal

The card catalogue of Olin Library, the main library of Cornell University, lists 102 entries under the subject of "equality," another 69 entries under the subject of "equal opportunity," and a mere 11 entries under the subject of "inequality." This lopsided distribution, heavily weighted toward "equality" by more than 15 to 1, symbolizes the orientation that Americans have held toward the subject and probably still do. There has been a clear preference to think positively in terms of an ideal goal rather than to face up to the negative realities of inequality. Illogical as it may sound, many people are adamantly "for" equality but are without concern for inequality of matching intensity. Perhaps it is because the first can be satisfied by making periodic declarations of allegiance, while the second implies awareness that leads to some action. To grasp the subtlety of this difference is to begin understanding the elements contained in America's traditional belief in equality.

FACING UP TO INEQUALITY

The emphasis upon "equality" over "inequality" apparently allows us to hold on to the ideal without facing the contradictions that daily experiences with inequality continue to produce. Thereby, we have been able to avoid that close look at the realities of inequality while we console ourselves by our reiterated dedication to the search for equality. Such a stance could explain, for example, the long period of acceptance of the principle of "separate but equal" in education until the Supreme Court's rejection of the practice in 1954 as discriminatory and therefore unconstitutional. By labeling what clearly was an unequal practice as being "separate but equal," the majority of Americans could continue to believe that equality was not being jeopardized when, in fact, it was being violated to the very core.

The same stance was also evident in the "war on poverty," which was initiated by stressing the goal of "equal opportunity," yet with only a glancing mention of the inequalities that made the poverty programs necessary. The first sentence of the Economic Opportunities Act of 1964 reads: "Although the economic well-being and prosperity of the United States have progressed to a level surpassing any achieved in world history, and although these benefits are widely shared throughout the Nation, poverty continues to be the lot of a substantial number of our people." Reading this statement of purpose, one might wonder why any action was deemed necessary since such a high level of progress had been achieved. Since we were this good, why bother any more?

RACIAL AND ECONOMIC INEQUALITY

As much as any other events, the 1954 Supreme Court decision and the 1964 Economic Opportunities Act have both forced a greater sensitivity toward racial and economic inequalities. Whether we like it or not, we have been forced to move beyond the simple affirmations of support for equality and have been forced to bypass the simplistic view of inequality as meaning only overt discrimination. What Americans have been learning since 1954 is that each corrective action taken against some manifestation of inequality uncovers yet additional features that were not previously considered. For instance, the efforts to correct school segregation have opened up the complex problems of discriminatory education, residential segregation, and neighborhood control of schools. The efforts to correct the glaring violations of voter registration rights have opened up the deeper discrimination involved in citizens' rights on jury panels and in their rights regarding police actions. We have come to learn that racial inequalities can be perpetuated even as we believe that we are moving actively against them. The lesson, quite simply, is that the imposition of equal practices upon historically unequal conditions does not lead automatically toward the desired goal. For example, open college admissions may indeed be determined without regard to race or financial status, but that action alone can hardly correct the years of inferior education for the blacks and the poor so as to permit them to compete equally for entrance into college. This dilemma becomes compounded, then, for we are reluctant to try inequality in the opposite direction by admitting a fixed proportion of minority group applicants into college regardless of their ability. When some colleges try open admissions procedures, others appeal to what are thought to be imperiled academic standards. Decades of inequality cannot be so quickly corrected.

Much the same sort of dilemma arises in the case of economic inequality as well. Poverty is immediately the result of having less money than others, but it is also very much the result of being locked out of the educational, occupational, and economic advantages open to most other Americans. The "war on poverty" is being lost because we do not care to sustain a high level of commitment of our resources to attack the problems at their core. Further, we are reluctant to practice inequality in order to assure some of the advantages to the poor, especially as others had to compete and sacrifice for these advantages. Those who have struggled to stay above the poverty level have no patience or understanding for programs that would reward those who have not, in their view, even tried. Yet, it has become evident that without special aid little can be done to resolve the inequalities of poverty, and as an alternative, many Americans would prefer to believe that the poor deserve what they get because of some personal failing.

Still, a measure of the progress we have made in the last twenty years is that these more subtle evidences of inequality no longer are novel or unexpected. The earlier expectations that most inequalities could be resolved either by a simple declaration of purpose or by prohibiting discrimination in overt form have been replaced by a deeper awareness of the social realities involved. Equality, we are being forced to recognize, can be achieved only through a serious and sustained reallocation of society's resources and opportunities. We can no longer assume that the system will operate automatically to correct social inequalities because we declare our ideal to be one of equal opportunities for all citizens. To have learned even this much represents a significant advance over earlier decades.

PROGRESS TOWARD AFFIRMATIVE GOALS

Pessimists may despair of making any advances, but by contrast with earlier beliefs and conditions, American society has come some way toward the positive goals it has so long proclaimed. Less than twenty years ago, if the Supreme Court's decision in 1954 is taken as the base line, most Americans still assumed that the system was automatically self-correcting, and at the same time, that some discrimination and inequality were inevitable, necessary, and even fair. It was not so long ago, then, that these views were personified in a tidy parcel of social axioms: Indians belonged on reservations; talented blacks had as much chance for success as whites; the institutionally supported lynchings of blacks in the South and the systematic denial of civil rights elsewhere were wrong, but either there was not much to be done about them or those people probably deserved it; poor people deserved poverty because they were lazy and would not plan ahead; since women were biologically different from men, they could not expect equal treatment in other spheres of life; some racial and religious discrimination did exist, but we could not change that because people have a right to run their own affairs and live their lives as they choose. The conventional wisdom, as usual, simply rationalized the prevailing practices and gave them an aura of timeless validity.

Challenges to Tradition

Obviously, much of this has changed in the last two decades. Indians occupied Alcatraz for a time to symbolize the unequal treatment they have suffered, and they have challenged the government in the courts to sue for their historic rights. Blacks, militant and otherwise, have challenged the prevailing patterns of discrimination and have demanded effective equality in education, employment, housing, and other sectors of life. Women have gained legal support for equal pay and equal employment and now are moving to question a series of assumptions about their inferior social status as established by men. Even the poor, the least organized of any of these groups, have achieved some public recognition of their existence so that they are not so automatically pushed aside and forgotten. In many areas of American life that bear directly upon the conditions of equality and inequality, then, the seemingly timeless assumptions and beliefs have been scrutinized and are being evaluated anew.

Such positive changes, I believe, are part of broader changes that have been taking place in American society. Whatever the depths of one's pessimism about such matters, there have been significant improvements in attitudes, beliefs, and practices. Primary among these is the perceptible increase in personal freedom that has become evident over the past two decades, although this is not an unmixed trend as I shall show shortly.

Increased Personal Freedom

Greater personal freedom lies at the core of effective equality and, indeed, can be equated almost perfectly with it. Although we usually talk about equality in terms of groups—the blacks, the poor, women, Chicanos—the realization of this equality comes with the opportunities opened up for individuals. Hence, racial and economic inequalities are counteracted when persons are treated as individuals rather than as undistinguished members of some grouping. An absolute minimum for achieving equality, then, is to consider individuals on their separate merits rather than stereotyping them with the presumed characteristics of an entire group. By this line of reasoning, the advances made in maximizing personal freedom (in other words, enhancing the separate role of the individual) also lead toward the development of social equality. As soon as we can stop thinking of "the poor" or "the blacks" as homogeneous groups, then we can begin to increase the area of freedom available to the individuals included in those groups.

Clearly, this movement toward greater freedom of choice means that there are also institutional changes as well, for I do not wish to leave the impression that all that is required is that people change their way of thinking. Laws, court decisions, executive orders and similar actions that legitimately alter our institutional practices are critical for creating a broader sector of choice and enforcing it. When persons accused of a crime are guaranteed their rights to avoid self-incrimination, when the power of censorship is restricted, or when a black child is given the opportunity to attend a school formerly closed to him, then we can appreciate the importance of such changes in our institutional procedures for maximizing personal freedoms. Such changes, in short, serve to prevent the use of a group as the reference level and instead open the way for individual judgments and evaluations. It is along such paths that social equality must be pursued; and it has been along some of these paths that important changes have taken place in American society in the last two decades.

Not very long ago, for example, a bearded poet, Allen Ginsburg, got a lot of publicity for campaigning in the nude to legalize marijuana. The whole thing seemed quite preposterous at the time, both in manner and in substance. Yet, since then not only have beards and public nudity become common enough, but also the argument for legalizing marijuana no longer sounds so improbable.

Consider, too, the changing attitudes toward the war in Indochina. Recall that the first few who dared to challenge America's involvement automatically were treated as traitors and draft-dodgers. As in every war beginning with the Revolution, there have been those who objected, but they usually were overwhelmed by a strong surge of patriotism that stifled dissent. This has not happened with Vietnam, where quite the opposite, our continued involvement has generated greater dissent, from the streets to the chamber of Congress.

Both examples illustrate the kind of changes that have broadened the range of choice for many Americans. There are others, such as the easing of sexual mores that allow for greater choice in what we can choose to read, see, and do; legal abortions, more widespread and more public support for contraception and family planning; easing of divorce laws; and an easier acceptance of heterosexual relations as well as homosexual behavior on college campuses and elsewhere. The undeniable effect of these changes has been to increase individual choice, and thereby, individual freedom. Such changes are an integral part of our changing beliefs concerning equality and inequality by which we have been more concerned with the deeper implications of equality rather than with overt inequality alone. We have begun to discover that the prohibition of overt discrimination is not the end of the search for equality, but rather, that it must continue to the creation of as much effective personal freedom and choice as is possible.

LOOKING AHEAD

It would be false and naive to commend ourselves on the progress we have made and to settle back righteously and contentedly. As will be elucidated throughout this book, there is still some distance to go, and what must count is next year as well as last year. Even as some areas of choice have been opened, we have moved also in the opposite direction to close other areas and to narrow the permissible range of dissent by penalizing those who depart too far from what are believed to be the prevailing views of the majority. For example, Leslie Fiedler, an American literary critic writing about his experiences of being busted by a charge of maintaining premises (his own home) where marijuana was used, tells of having his home-owner insurance canceled by practically every company as a bad moral risk and having his financial credit withdrawn as though a total blacklist existed.[1] Harassment and penalties still are experienced by homosexuals if they venture too far out into the straight world. Surveillance of all manner of so-called suspicious and undesirable persons by federal agencies (including members of scientific review panels) and by credit companies that apparently exchange their information can hardly be considered as a force for increasing the freedom of individual choice. So, change in both directions is occurring at the same time.

Action and Reaction

Let us also remember that the price of the progress we have made in shaking some of our earlier convictions about inequality and freedom has resulted in a threat to the stability of those newfound beliefs. Hence, there is the constant likelihood that older beliefs will reemerge even more strongly as new events shake our sense of security. For example, the majority of white Americans who had accepted the efforts to reduce racial discrimination may well reach a limit after which they retreat to earlier prejudices and practices because their own favored status is threatened. In fact, a number already have retreated. Black Americans, on the other hand, have tasted some success and are hardly inclined to quit or to slow the pace of change, let alone to return to some earlier state. The point to be stressed is that such changes carry with them their own dynamics and their own contradictions. We are not dealing with a mechanical process by which individuals simply shed one set of beliefs and then adopt another. Instead, actions create reactions in Newtonian fashion so that the course of change becomes erratic and variable rather than being a single, straight-line progression without deviations.

However, no matter what the trends may be at any given moment, I believe that it is impossible to return simply to the earlier condition as if nothing had happened. To once recognize that racial and economic inequalities exist, to begin doing something about them, and to agree that they are not inevitable all close the path of return to an exact duplication of any earlier conditions. This is not to say that inequality is forever dropped from our social lexicon, but rather that new interpretations and variations on older beliefs have to be devised if the situation requires it.

My point in all of this is not to try to balance the weights of the opposing forces for greater freedom and equality on the one side, as against greater restriction and inequality on the other. Rather, it is to keep before us the fact that such changes contain both positive and negative elements; in effect, each action generates reaction. Therefore, there is no simple arithmetic that will reveal to us just how far we have come or just how far we have yet to go. In fact, it is the primary task of this book to describe and analyze the elements that are involved in trying to make such assessments. Later, I will consider what this means specifically for racial and for economic inequalities, but let me indicate briefly some of the general factors that are involved.

Judging Various Trends

For one thing, it is virtually impossible to make an objective evaluation of the opposing trends so as to reach an unambiguous conclusion. In addition, there is a wide latitude of interpretation concerning how much inequality we have on the one hand and how much equality we can attain on the other. Those who are reasonably satisfied with what they have are likely to compare the present with the past and to read improvements into every effort that has been made. By contrast, those who have suffered most from such inequalities are likely to compare the present with an ideal future and to be more pessimistic and dissatisfied.

For another thing, it is very difficult to assess the depths of the changes that have occurred, which is to say that it is not easy to determine how lasting and meaningful they are. In the words of Orlando Fals Borda,[2] it is a question of determining whether the changes are *significant* or *marginal.* The first occurs "when variations in the components of social order call for adjustments in the existing patterns of value dominance and the collective aims of society." By contrast, marginal change occurs "when modifications in the components of the social order are either partial or minor, so that the value system is not inherently in question." Marginal changes, such as raising the amount of welfare benefits by a fraction, may look like a progressive step but they really do almost nothing to disturb either the position of the poor or our beliefs about them. Significant changes, on the other hand, such as an effective and more equitably spread income distribution would alter the situation of economic inequality, but those changes are more difficult to effect. Clearly, an assessment of trends would require the recognition of such differences.

Finally, we are always faced with great difficulties whenever we attempt to assess the significance of changes as those changes are occurring. Looking backward, we might date the civil rights movement and the subsequent black movement to Mrs. Rosa Parks' reluctance to move to the back of the bus, or we might date the "war on poverty" to President Kennedy's night table copy of Harrington's book, *The Other America.*[3] To be sure, these are merely symbolic benchmarks for changes with roots extending more deeply into history, but few persons, if any, must have realized the full significance of what was happening at the time. For that matter, there must have been many incipiently significant changes that never got off the ground. In large measure, our assessments of the moment are very much a function of what we believe and what we wish to see happen. Depending upon age, affluence, and many other factors one is likely to be either shocked or dismayed at the pace and substance of the changes that are taking place today. I intend to bring some of these factors into focus as I describe the conditions of inequality.

THE SUBJECTIVE NATURE OF REACTION

The discussion of equality and inequality triggers personal ideologies and beliefs, and with them too, the contradictory nature of the subject itself. The value of equality for society is the availability of institutional means for recognizing talent and rewarding abilities without prejudgments based upon ascribed criteria such as sex, race, ethnicity, age, or religion. Presumably, then, society gets the best talent it can to conduct its activities. This, essentially, is the grounding for our belief in social equality. Yet, counterposed to this belief is the reluctance to allow it full play because it carries the potential threat to the security and stability of one's position, especially if that position is an advantageous one. Whoever reaches the top of the hill would prefer to have the game stopped right then, or at least, to change the rules so that no one else can challenge his position. The institutional supports of male superiority, for instance, effectively cut down competition from those women who may be equally, if not more talented, than their male counterpart. Similarly, the institutional supports of white superiority reduce most of the competition from blacks by closing off the channels for them to actively question the arrangement. Inequality, therefore, has positive advantages for those who benefit from it; the beneficiaries, at the same time, are able to exert the most power to keep institutional arrangements the same as they were.

A SNEAK PREVIEW

In the rest of this book, I will consider in detail what has been happening with blacks and with the poor as the personification of the two principal manifestations of inequality. We will examine the issue of whether recent changes have had any marked or lasting effect upon the existing patterns of inequality. At this point, however, let me sketch briefly some of the broad changes that have taken place.

As I mentioned earlier, we have little cause to rest content with the changes that have occurred and little cause to believe that all problems have been solved. In fact, as a society we have come off pretty badly when one considers the decades during which we really evaded a sustained effort to translate our beliefs into practice. Even so, it is significant for our future that in so short a period of time (especially compared with the previous period of almost total inaction) the movement toward greater racial equality has jumped beyond such peripheral issues as the integration of travelers' facilities in waiting rooms and restaurants to such central issues as employment, education, housing and the like. Both the level of the demands and the substance of the debates have been greatly elevated in comparison with earlier years. Similarly, we are much less inclined than previously to condemn the poor because we believe that they are lazy and lacking in ambition and in talent. Instead, we have begun at least to distinguish between different types and causes of poverty and to consider ways of overcoming the inherent poverty-based disabilities that are laid upon the poor. We have begun to recognize that we must stop "blaming the victim" (to use one of William Ryan's[4] phrases). That concept has brought us closer to understanding inequality as a social fault.

Still, neither in the case of racial inequality nor in the case of economic inequality have we progressed as far as we might, let alone as far as we should have progressed. We are still far from having unplugged the institutional channels to allow for able and talented poor and blacks to rise. Yet, what general assessement can be made at this time about our continued progress toward the goal of equality? What are the grounds for optimism, if any?

Certainly, any optimism about the future for equality must be tempered by social realities. Social inequality is as old as human history, as universal as human societies. Everywhere and in every epoch there has existed some form of stratification with those at the top holding more privilege, power, and enjoying greater rewards than those at the bottom. Inequality, not equality, has been the predominant social rule by which most men at most times have lived. The rationales used by those in power to explain and justify inequality have varied throughout human history, even as the effects have turned out to be remarkably similar. In this, as in most other areas of social existence, the explanations given to justify inequality have revealed the remarkable imagination of people both to construct such explanations and to accept them as reasonable. In one form or another, and at different times, God, the supernatural, nature, blood, tradition, and science have been used to explain why some system of stratification exists and why it is proper for some members of a society to have so much while others have less. In our own time, when justifications such as blood lines, heavenly choice, and social Darwinism are more or less rejected, most Americans still are quite prepared to accept explanations that trace social success to ambition, native abilities, and a dedication to hard work.* By this view, the circumstances into which people are born and in which they mature, apparently, have relatively little to do with it. Our explanations conveniently account for those who are successful as well as for the failures; all in all, a secular and modern version of the Calvinist doctrine of predestination.

The United States, the most affluent country in the world, has about 12 percent of the population classified as poor—about 24 million persons. I have no doubts that for many, if not most Americans, this juxtaposition of poverty and affluence represents justice in that most of the poor, seen from above, deserve their poverty. Inequality, thereby, becomes a natural social phenomenon and one to be expected because of the differences among individuals.

---

*The culture hero of hard work continues to remain a culture hero. Harold S. Geneen, chairman and chief executive of the International Telephone & Telegraph Corporation at an annual salary of $766,000, often works 20 hours a day and "has virtually sacrificed his personal life to build I.T.T. to its present position." *New York Times*, September 5, 1971.

THE ELUSIVE DREAM

Pessimism about equality is based also on the recognition that there has never been a time when any society has achieved social equality for a sustained period. To be sure, the social forms have been changed in the search, and monarchies have fallen beneath the banner of intended equality. Yet, the result has been that new social hierarchies have emerged in their turn with newer brands of inequalities and a different, but unequal, redistribution of rewards and privileges. A few attempts at perfect equality in utopian colonies in the last century and some of the present-day hippie colonies do not increase one's optimism about attaining that goal for larger numbers. Also, some societies have proclaimed equality, including the U.S., the Soviet Union, and Israel, but even they have not lived up to their claims. They can be credited with enunciating the formal objective, using the rhetoric of equality, and perhaps even trying. But the attainment of equality, in fact, is quite another matter that easily can elude the rhetoric and sincerity of motives, as will be discussed later.

INEQUALITY AS A SOCIAL PROBLEM

With so much evidence, past and present, why should social inequality be considered a social problem at all? Why, in other words, be concerned about poverty, about racial discrimination, or about ethnic prejudice when the attainment of equality appears to be so unlikely? I ask the question because the term *social problem* not only must refer to some feature that is thought to be undesirable in a society but also must be adjudged capable of solution or relief. In addition, I would add a third element: that the problem must affect a significantly large number of persons if it is to be a *social* problem.

The first and last defining elements are self-evident. If a situation is not undesirable, then it can hardly be considered a problem. Furthermore, if the situation does not affect a large number of people, then it is not social. Aunt Minny may be a problem to her relatives, but she does not represent a social problem unless she is part of a class of people who have the specific problem, such as alcoholics, the aged, the mentally ill, or those who have whatever Aunt Minny's problem seems to be. From a political point of view, a social problem that is geographically widespread throughout the country is more likely to be recognized and possibly acted upon than one that is geographically concentrated. For example, the problem of racial inequality is a case in point. As long as the majority of blacks were concentrated in a few southern states, relatively little pressure was exerted upon the majority of whites, there or elsewhere, to think of race as a problem requiring their attention. Of course, some voices both within and outside the region were raised in protest, but the political forces that condoned inequality in the South were insensitive to any such clamor. Nor did they have to be any different. W. J. Cash in his book, *The Mind of the South,* which still remains as a classic sociological description of the region around the time of World War I, isolates very nicely the tight social control that prevented racial inequality from surfacing as a problem.

Contrary to widespread popular belief, which the South itself has fostered, the persistence of lynching in the region down to the present [1941] has not been due simply and wholly to the white-trash classes. Rather, the major share of the responsibility in all those areas where the practice has remained common rests squarely on the shoulders of the master classes. The common whites have usually done the actual execution, of course, though even that is not an invariable rule. . . . But they have kept on doing it, in the last analysis, only because their betters either consented quietly or, more often, definitely approved.[5]

The postwar migration of blacks out of the rural South and into the urban North, however, served to implicate and thereby involve many more Americans than before. Southern politicians who offered free one-way bus fare to dissatisfied blacks wanting to leave the South knew what they were doing. Racial problems, thereby, became national in scope rather than remaining regional.

The second element I mentioned above, that of a possible solution or relief, is less obvious perhaps as a defining criterion of a social problem, but it is the most important. If some condition of society is considered as undesirable, there has to be a companion belief that something can be done about it, otherwise we cannot speak of a social problem. Death, for example, is not a social problem in this meaning of the word even though all societies have institutional provisions for reestablishing the importance of the social group after a death. Insanity, to take another example, was not a social problem until relatively late when we stopped defining it as the result of witchcraft, bad humors, or the devil. Closer to the subject at hand, race was not a social problem as long as blacks were slaves, or even later, were thought to be biologically inferior to whites. You cannot argue with biology or nature. Yet, it is also true that science can counteract ignorance by revealing that what was thought to be biological or natural is indeed social and thereby capable of remedy. I believe that the reluctance of some Americans to consider either poverty or race as social problems stems from their belief that biology rather than society is responsible for these inequalities.

Even so, economic and racial inequalities have existed for a long time, have been justified by persuasive nonsocial arguments, and have nowhere been overcome. Indeed, one may well wonder why they should be considered as social problems that are capable of solution or remedy. In the light of history, is it not reasonable to conclude that inequality is an inevitable and inescapable condition of social existence? Apparently not, because misguided or not, Americans have tried in the last decade to solve it by dedicating a considerable amount of their resources.

Why, indeed, have Americans even bothered to try? After all, they have for decades believed that social inequalities were corrected automatically by the normal functioning of their institutional system. Those inequalities that did exist were legitimate consequences of that system, and therefore, it was unnecessary to tamper or intervene with its functioning. De Tocqueville was among the first to give expression to this belief, so entranced was he with the American experiment in social equality. "No novelty in the United States," he wrote in his introduction, "struck me more vividly during my stay there than the equality of conditions. It was easy to see the immense influence of this basic fact on the whole course of society. It gives a particular turn to public opinion and a particular twist to the laws, new maxims to those who govern and particular habits to the governed."[6] And later on: "It is not that in the United States as everywhere, there are no rich; indeed I know of no other country where love of money has such a grip on men's hearts or where stronger scorn is expressed for the theory of permanent equality of property. But wealth circulates there with incredible rapidity, and experience shows that two successive generations seldom enjoy its favors."[7]*

Even more recently, a number of American social scientists have been contending that the spirit and validity of de Tocqueville's analysis are still alive. They share the highly optimistic tone that Seymour Martin Lipset expressed in his historical analysis of America. "American values, more than those of other nations, have encouraged men to apply equalitarian and achievement orientations to the polity and its various institutions. . . . [T]he fact that this New Nation has succeeded in fostering economic growth and democracy under the aegis of equalitarian values holds out hope for the rest of the world."[8]

This tone is reiterated in the conclusions of some economists who

*De Tocqueville, I must add, did not see everything in America as an unmixed blessing, nor did he accept uncritically the pursuit of equality as good. Regarding the first point: "When all the privileges of birth and fortune are abolished, when all professions are accessible to all, and a man's own energies may place him at the top of any one of them, an easy and unbounded career seems open to his ambition, and he will readily persuade himself that he is born to no vulgar destinies. . . . The same equality which allows every citizen to conceive these lofty hopes renders all the citizens less able to realize them: [I]t circumscribes their powers on every side, while it gives freer scope to their desires. . . . When men are nearly alike, and all follow the same track, it is very difficult for any one individual to walk quickly and cleave a way through the dense throng which surrounds and presses him." (Edition translated by Henry Reeve and edited by Henry Steele Commager. New York: Oxford University Press, 1947, p. 346.)

Regarding the second point: "Democratic peoples always like equality, but there are times when their passion for it turns to delirium. . . . At such times men pounce on equality as their booty and cling to it as a precious treasure they fear to have snatched away. The passion for equality seeps into every corner of the human heart, expands, and fills the whole. It is no use telling them that by this blind surrender to an exclusive passion they are compromising their dearest interests; they are deaf. It is no use pointing out that freedom is slipping from their grasp while they look the other way; they are blind, or rather they can see but one thing to covet in the whole world." (Doubleday Anchor Books, op. cit., p. 505.) For an unusual analysis of de Tocqueville's writings as a model description of social change, see Paul R. Eberts and Ronald A. Witton, "Recall from Anecdote: Alexis de Tocqueville and the Morphogenesis of America," *American Sociological Review*, 35 (December 1970), 1081–97.

read the statistics of income distribution in America as proof of a continuous trend toward the leveling of incomes. By their interpretation the upper income groups have been receiving a decreasing share of the available income, thereby allowing for those in the middle and at the bottom to earn more. Similarly, some sociologists have analyzed the occupational structure and have concluded that there is evidence of continued upward mobility (in other words, equal opportunities) in American society. When all allowances are made for the changes that have taken place in the occupational structure, they conclude that each generation has been improving its occupational position compared to the distribution for the preceding generation.

These interpretations of the constantly improving state of society fit in well with what most Americans probably believe. With respect to our views about individual freedoms, we began as a nation firmly grounded in the beliefs and values of the eighteenth century. Even though our world has changed considerably since then, there still remains more than a trace of those values in our present conceptions. There have been those who doubt such interpretations; yet the strength of our embrace of egalitarian values seems hardly to have been loosened as a result. Hence, there are some economists who read almost the same set of the above-mentioned statistics covering income distribution but who emerge with a much more pessimistic interpretation. This group sees a continued trend toward greater monopolization of income by upper groups. Similarly, some sociologists interpret the changes in occupational distribution as proof of greater occupational inheritance rather than continued upward mobility. As might be expected, these pessimistic economic and social views do not attract as much attention as the optimistic views because the latter confirm what we want to believe.

The object of this discussion is not the elaborate presentation of competing arguments and the deduction of their conclusions. The relevant point is that Americans have a long history of dedication to the value of equality, even to the extent of disregarding what the concrete conditions of the moment are like. Perhaps it is only faith, or perhaps it is more than that, but in either case the belief in equality intrudes into our consciousness and has a great deal to do with the way we define the current situation and the methods for correction that we would find acceptable.

It can be inferred from the above comments by de Tocqueville and others that there is a strong impetus behind the traditional belief in equality that accounts for the general willingness by Americans to try to overcome inequalities. A companion belief, as I have suggested, is that the institutional processes are self-correcting to the extent that existing inequalities will tend to be adjusted inasmuch as the values are basically sound. When confronted with clear evidence of large-scale poverty and racial discrimination, however, Americans at least are then forced to become consciously aware of their beliefs. Thus the pressures to confront the evidence have generated, as a minimum, a new recognition about inequality, and more importantly, some questioning and doubts about the self-correcting mechanisms. Even this minimal recognition is of considerable importance despite the fact that it may not produce immediate remedies to the problem of inequality.

THE LONG-OVERDUE ATTENTION FROM POLITICAL LEADERS

The point that needs to be made here is that the recognition of social inequalities by political leaders and by a large proportion of Americans has been a long time in coming. The Reconstruction Amendments—the abolition of slavery, the guarantee of citizenship rights, and equal rights—were not strongly enforced until the 1954 Supreme Court school integration decision in *Brown v. Board of Education* and later legislative and executive policy contained in the Civil Rights Act of 1964. "Separate but equal" remained the guiding philosophy until the 1954 decision even though there was plentiful evidence that the former interpretation in most cases was discriminatory. The rhetoric has changed to "freedom of choice," and, undoubtedly, other phrases will be developed in time. The fact remains, however, that racial equality in education and in other areas is not easy to achieve.

Poverty and its attendant economic inequalities took longer to recognize as a social problem, mainly because so many Americans seemed to be convinced that the economic mechanisms were functioning effectively. Furthermore, the recognition of the poor as a stable group would have meant a companion recognition of class structure, which Americans are averse to admitting. The dominant conception of America as a middle-class society was well supported by the belief in general economic affluence as part of our self-image through most of the decades after World War II. Even today, we try to evade a view of poverty couched in class terms, preferring to define the problem as one of individual failure or faulty socialization rather than as a structural failure. It is no wonder, then, that the recognition of economic inequality took so long in coming. This awareness dates back to the Economic Opportunity Act of 1964. Even though the Act was prefaced by an indictment of the nation's affluence, there was the formal recognition that poverty exists for some Americans. Yet, the mobilization of resources to combat poverty did not maintain the initial high peak, as was noted by S. M. Miller in his assessment of the response to the program a decade after its inception. "In a few short years, the United States suddenly discovered an enduring enemy and called it 'poverty'; then declared war on it, but restricted the weapons that were to be used in the pursuit of the enemy; rapidly proclaimed the goal of unconditional surrender; began to adduce skimpy battlefield communiqués of success before the regiments were properly marshaled; and then lost interest as another war, in a more distant land with a strange name, absorbed resources and attention."[9]

Can the Public Take the Credit?

What is revealing is that the formal recognition of inequality, although belated, came from the top leadership rather than from the public. Most Americans, being neither poor nor black, seemed to live in a state of general ignorance, having no cause to doubt the efficacy of their institutions. Staying within their own social worlds, most Americans could avoid the need to see inequalities except in the most transitory way. Moving within social enclosures—the suburb, the automobile, the office, the university—most Americans were isolated from direct contact with the consequences of inequality, and except for a passing glimpse, had no reason to see the underside of American society. Even the networks of insulated traffic corridors—the expressway and the freeway—have served effectively to keep Americans clear of any contact with the ghetto areas through which they might have to travel on their route between home and work, just as the tour bus insulates the traveler from that uncomfortable contact with the natives. Of course, this underside of American society was shown from time to time in pictures of race riots, in the statistics on income, and in some reports on poverty. However, these realities were sterilized by the printed page or the television tube and there was no effective social contact between strata. Because of the high value placed on equality, most Americans preferred to believe that the system was working well.

It is relatively easy to overlook social inequalities or to explain them away as the inevitable consequences of individual differences. After all, we never believed that all individuals were equal; we believed only that everyone had an equal opportunity to succeed—and to fail. Those at the bottom really must deserve their status because they are lazy, untalented, or evil. T. V. Smith has summarized this view very well. "There are, first, the stubborn facts. Men do not at first glance seem to be equal in any assignable manner. And what is more perturbing to the democrat, they do not seem any more equal on the sober second thought than at first glance. Indeed, the longer one thinks it over, the more certain does it become that men are not just what the term equality suggests. And the more specific the analysis, the more obvious the discrepancy."[10]

This line of reasoning has considerable appeal. It makes the judge appear more worthy to himself by comparison and all the more worthy if he has worked hard to succeed. People deserve what they get in an achievement-oriented society, which spells success for the worthy and failure for the others. That rationale has hardly changed in the 200 years or so it has been around.

When none of these explanations is acceptable, the individual is always free to escape into "realism"; that is, he can convince himself that there is little that can be done to correct inequalities because the "problem" is too massive and too complex. Responsibility for solutions, thereby, falls elsewhere, and especially upon those who are presumed to have the power to remedy the situation. Yet, it is this latter group that is the least likely to effect remedies unless circumstances force some sort of action.

It is doubtless that most, if not all, Americans consider themselves to be fair and unprejudiced. Even southern congressmen who for decades depended upon racial discrimination to elect them, speak freely of the many fine blacks whom they know and respect. Millions of Americans undoubtedly were morally shocked by the pictures of angry white mothers screaming at a lonely, black third-grader being escorted by federal marshals into a formerly all white school. Yet, these same millions have lived racially segregated lives themselves, apparently without serious qualms. And, if there are qualms, well what, after all, can one person do to correct such massive injustices?

The last question raises another relevant issue: Just how willing are Americans to consider economic and racial inequalities as *their* problem? Do they, in fact, consider these inequalities to be undesirable features of American society; secondly, do they consider that action can and should be taken to correct them; and thirdly, how much will they spend and surrender to reach for solutions?

Will Progress Continue?

As far as race is concerned, there are indications that the white majority already has become reluctant to pursue further remedies. I discern a growing sentiment that we have done enough for the moment with voting rights, some school integration, and a handful of economic measures. What has now appeared is a white reaction to the strident demands of black militants and others for quota hiring, reparations, and further school integration; yet there seems to be a sense of indignation at the separatism that is contained explicitly in many of the demands by blacks. For working-class whites, the black demands for employment are excessive because they threaten and mock their efforts to achieve economic security and respectability. For intellectuals, the black demands for segregation are an affront to their favorite ideologies.

A DIFFERENT PERSPECTIVE

Until now, I have been discussing inequality as a social problem seen from the top; in other words, from the majority's point of view. Those at the bottom who meet the effects of inequality head-on also may be able to influence the outcome of the situation; after all, they are not always passive. The power to define social problems is not the exclusive prerogative of those at the top, who incidentally, usually are satisfied with the way things are going. Rather, among the several social strata in a society there is always the possibility of interchange by which those at the bottom can make their position known and may induce action by those who can exert power. In the extreme case, revolution or revolt generated at the bottom by those suffering the inequalities can destroy or significantly modify the existing institutional structure. In less extreme cases, the institutional structure can be modified and altered in order to achieve a new and possibly different balance. Although the majority and its leadership may be reluctant to alter existing arrangements, it may become the case that they must make changes if they are to retain power. None of these responses, however, is automatic or preordained as some social theorists might contend. Rather, into each concrete situation there enters a variety of complex factors that finally determine the direction and scope of the changes that are eventually effected.

Applying this perspective to the situation of the poor in the U.S., it must be concluded that there is little real power concentrated here. The number of those living below the poverty level certainly is large. If numbers alone determined power, then the poor would represent a force with which to reckon. They, however, are not a homogeneous group—a condition which dilutes what otherwise could be a strong power base. Some 30 percent are nonwhite and their destinies are more effectively tied to race than to an economic class. Another significant proportion includes those with an inadequate income such as many of the elderly and the infirm. Obviously, their needs are quite different from those who are younger and who are able to work but who are either unemployed or underemployed. Another segment includes the poor in rural areas. In short, there is no single social dimension—other than poverty—that can provide a unifying force for this highly heterogeneous group. They are heterogeneous, geographically dispersed, and without any indigenous leadership; it seems clear that the poor in the U.S. are largely dependent upon others from outside their stratum to make a case for them. It should also be noted that most persons who do succeed in escaping are not likely to maintain any identification with it, so that the poor are all the less likely to develop strong leaders.

The situation is different for the matter of race. Among blacks there is a solid and visible basis for identification upon which to develop a strong group consciousness. The poor black and the affluent black can and do join together by virtue of race, so that what helps one can well help the other. The situation is strongly aided, too, by the physical proximity imposed by the urban ghetto which serves to bring large numbers of blacks together. Of course, physical proximity by itself is not enough, just as numbers are not enough to create organization and consciousness. Yet, added to the basis for a common identification, proximity and numbers do become significant. Not only is it easier to organize power, but also it is easier to use the power, whether through institutional channels such as voting, or through riot and rebellion. The recognition of racial inequality as a social problem, therefore, has come about not only through the good graces of white leadership, important as this was, but because blacks have made their inequality into a national social problem.[11]

I do not want to leave the impression, even at this early point in the analysis, that black success is automatic. Obviously, it is not. For one thing, there is evidence of continuing struggles between the leadership of black organizations so that there is always less than consensus or unity of action. For another thing, there are varying levels of involvement and interest among black citizens themselves in the interests of racial equality. In other words, there is more than one black community even within a city, although outsiders think there is but one. Those black persons who have been economically successful, either through inheritance or through their own efforts, have not always remained tied to the black cause, and they reject militancy as a threat to their own favored position. Finally, the reaction by white majorities is coming to be felt more and more, so that the gains that have been made in the past ten years or so should not be taken as a sound basis to extrapolate the trends for the future. Middle-class and lower-class whites, particularly, are showing signs that they have gone about as far as they are willing to go in giving up their privileges so as to help redress the racial imbalances. They are even less inclined to do so when inflation, growing unemployment, and other manifestations of economic insecurity become real.

AN OVERVIEW

In this introductory chapter I have attempted to inventory some of the complex variables that need to be considered when analyzing the social problems of economic and racial inequality. Above all, perhaps, the reader should keep in mind that these are socially dynamic variables that are constantly changing as different forces within a society come into play. The very attempt to attain social equality, it should be remembered, is itself a dynamic process.

2
Some Problems with Equality

A society that is dedicated to the attainment of social equality can expect problems and conflicts as a result. The reason, quite simply, is that there is a discrepancy between the equality ideal and the realities of inequality that is always present as a basis for dissatisfactions and for possible conflicts. As I have pointed out before, the barriers in the way of attaining equality in any society are considerable, so that there is a high probability that some inequalities will be present as a potential rationale for action. However, such discrepancies by themselves do not automatically generate conflicts—either because they are not recognized as unusual or because such recognition is not translated into social action.

CONFLICT VERSUS PEACE

It should be realized that the U.S. has never achieved its ideal, though its formal dedication to equality certainly is well known and is thoroughly emphasized in American values. Even so, the existence of inequalities has not generated long and continuous conflict as might be supposed. Yet, it is true that we have had times of mass violence created and fed by inequalities. The summer of 1967 was marked by riots in the black ghettos of Newark and Detroit. Just two years earlier, the Watts riot in Los Angeles was violent and destructive. It was the first of several "long hot summers" of bitter racial conflict. Earlier in our history there were mass race riots in the years surrounding each world war. There were smaller, but deadly, conflicts in Mississippi and Alabama arising from the civil rights movements in the late 1950s. Violence, generated by economic inequalities was the cause of the Haymarket riot of 1886. Economic inequalities were also the cause of the incidents arising from the organizing efforts of the Industrial Workers of the World at the beginning of this century and of the fledgling labor unions in the late 1930s. In this kind of inventory, one does not even begin to count the thousands of separate acts of lynchings, murders, and assassinations across race and class divisions—acts that had their bases in inequalities and the fear of change. Not counted either are the threats of violence and other threats that may have served to keep protests against existing inequalities from reaching a significant stage of action. Certainly, ours has not been a peaceful history.

The Low Level of Open Conflict

Still, one might ask why there were not even more social erruptions than these. Why, even now, after several decades of stress upon existing racial and economic discrimination, has there been more peace than revolt, more acceptance of existing conditions than violent rejection of them. Obviously, the answer is complex, but perhaps some elements of such an answer can be specified.

First, conflict is less likely to develop when most individuals believe that the discrepancy between the ideal of equality and the reality of inequality either is temporary or is being narrowed. Throughout most of our history, I suspect, the majority has been convinced that something was being done about the more flagrant inequalities and that such inequalities would be corrected in time. With this attitude, individuals simply are not going to become committed to a violent struggle to try to change things.

Second, conflict is not likely to develop as long as most individuals accept the inequalities that exist as being fair or justified. For instance, slaves were clearly not equal to white, free men, but then, such inequality was not considered to be any violation of the equality ideal as defined. Today, as long as the poor or the blacks are thought to deserve their status, then these manifestations of inequalities can be rationalized.

Third, even if individuals are persuaded that inequalities do exist, that they are unfair, and that they will not be improved automatically, they still must be convinced that open struggle and conflict will produce the desired results. For most, if not all, individuals this means that the legitimate channels for social change (the courts, voting, or letters to congressmen) are preferred to the dangers and uncertainties of open rebellion and riots. Lacking this conviction, some individuals can pursue nonviolent dissent of whatever form in order to try to effect changes. Even though it easily gets out of hand once begun, open revolt is not easy to generate.

Finally, even if all of the above conditions are met, there is still the great difficulty of bringing unity to mob actions because of the different complaints, different levels of personal intensity felt about those complaints, and different degrees of willingness to participate. For example, the studies of those who participated in the 1967 riots have revealed that many of these differences did exist. There was a variety of grievances held by blacks against whites, and with different levels of intensity, so that sizable numbers of ghetto residents did not participate in the riots that were exploding around them.[1]

Violence As the Exception

Each of these elements, and others as well, is necessary if open violence is to occur. Clearly, the fact that they have not always come together in the past explains why continuous violence over existing inequalities has not characterized most of American history. A more measured conclusion, therefore, is the one presented by the National Commission on the Causes and Prevention of Violence[2] that found there have been periods of calm and periods of violence linked to the recognition of existing social inequalities. The fact of such inequalities alone is not sufficient to explain why social erruptions occur. Rather, the entire social setting at the time must be considered, and even then, predictions are impossible to make with any accuracy. The powder keg may be there, but it is neither regularly nor predictably ignited.

An important feature of that setting is the depth of the challenge that is made against existing institutions, which can explain both the intensity of conflict for change and the resulting reaction against it. When the struggle for change, even in the name of equality, seriously attacks existing institutional mechanisms (presumably also dedicated to equality), then the resulting conflicts can be expected to be most severe. This is not a simple reflex action, but rather an action that can initiate repercussions throughout the entire social structure. For example, the apparently simple reform to achieve voting rights for blacks in the South became a real and immediate threat to local political control that long had been dominated by whites who were outnumbered. Consequently, all other relationships that depended upon political control were endangered, such as the allocation of federal funds for education, for poverty programs, and the like.

Violence and threats of violence that had been used for years to maintain white control were heightened as a result of the insistence by the federal government on equal voting rights. Blacks and their white supporters were systematically threatened to stay away from the polls until more federal pressure through court actions and federally appointed voting registrars was imposed. What may have been at the beginning a seemingly simple and long overdue solution has become instead the basis for some reallocation of political power, but still along relatively rigid, racial lines.

Similarly strong pressures, violence, and counterviolence also have characterized the gradual movement toward public school integration; a problem of inequality that is far from settled. Basic social values and beliefs on both sides of the race line are involved, which is why violent confrontations are so much a part of this issue—a condition that is hardly alleviated by signs from the executive branch of government for less stringent enforcement of earlier court guidelines. White parents feel that the quality of their children's education is being threatened by the mass introduction of black students into formerly all-white schools through integration formulas, and with it the chances for their children to enter college. Black parents feel that their children have been suffering from an inferior education for a long time and, wanting the same goals as white parents, are prepared to push their demands strongly. In some instances, black parents have demanded not integration into white schools, but instead, a greater measure of control over the schools their children are attending and an opportunity to improve their quality. The point is that education touches upon such basic values that most efforts to introduce equality must contend with deep beliefs and must generate extreme reactions. By contrast, for example, integration of lunch counters and public transportation was practically without incident in many formerly segregated communities. The incidents that did occur may have been automatic reactions to the novelty of the idea, as much as anything else. Perhaps there were also feelings of threat to established patterns. Still, these reactions did not persist with anything near the tenacity or strength of the often violent reactions to school integration. The furor that was created because a tired, elderly black woman refused to move to the back of the bus in Montgomery, or a bit later because Lester Maddox brandished an axe handle in front of his Atlanta restaurant against blacks trying to enter, is very much past us. As initial acts in the movement toward equality, they were noteworthy; but, as far as the institutional structure is concerned, they did not really pose a threat of the same order of magnitude as the search for equality in education, voting, employment, or housing.

THE DILEMMA OF EQUALITY

Let me return to the main issue with which I began this discussion: that the source of inequality problems can be traced to the discrepancy between the ideal of equality and the reality of inequality.

The admirable dedication to the ideal of equality by Americans always has contained the seeds of a moral dilemma—one which becomes apparent when the ideal must be tested against social reality. Probably Gunnar Myrdal, better than most commentators, has stated the essential nature of this dilemma:

. . . [A]t bottom our problem is the moral dilemma of the American—the conflict between his moral valuations on various levels of consciousness and generality. The "American Dilemma" . . . is the ever-raging conflict between, on the one hand, the valuations preserved on the general plane which we shall call the "American Creed," where the American thinks, talks, and acts under the influence of the high national and Christian precepts, and, on the other hand, the valuations on specific planes of individual and group living, where personal and local interests; economic, social, and sexual jealousies; considerations of community prestige and conformity; group prejudice against particular persons or types of people; and all sorts of miscellaneous wants, impulses, and habits dominate his outlook.[3]

There has been a tendency—erroneous I believe—to interpret Myrdal's statement of the "American Dilemma" as a static condition of American morality. The implication is that there is a hard line of separation between the ideals of equality on the one hand, and the realistic practices of inequality on the other. Not only is that a misinterpretation of Myrdal's ideas, but also it is a misreading of the nature of equality itself. Myrdal has defined the dilemma as an "ever-raging conflict," one which must be dynamic and changing. It is this feature, above all, that must be grasped: that equality is a *process,* not an absolute state or condition.

Equality As a Process

Equality is not an absolute state to be reached as is reaching the top of a mountain. Whether or not a society wishes to make the climb is a value it holds, but it must be recognized that equality does not exist as some final plateau which can be attained. Equality is a process in the sense that its definitions necessarily keep changing, thereby reflecting changing circumstances, including better social knowledge and understanding. Obviously, what seemed like a definitive statement of equality to the signers of the Declaration of Independence could not be accepted as adequate today; we know more about society and its structure than the signers ever could have known. Jefferson and his cosigners clearly did not mean to include their slaves when they declared that "all men are created equal." Even later, we learned that legal equality was not being enforced in the courts, let alone in the more informal social relationships of daily life, although we somehow assumed that enforcement would follow the law exactly. Recent court decisions, for example, have revealed the various ways by which the poor have been denied their legal rights (for example, by not being informed about them), as well as how blacks are denied equal treatment in the courts (for example, by underrepresentation on jury panels).

Equality, therefore, is never a final or absolute state. For one thing as the above examples were meant to illustrate, there is slippage between what ought to be and what, in fact, does exist. For another thing, social conditions change, and so also do the meanings of equality and what might be thought of as the acceptable limits of inequality. Equality is not a climb to the top of a mountain, but rather it is as if in climbing one mountain we discover new and unforeseen parts of the range that were not visible before, and that now require even higher ascent. Nor is it likely, in my view, that we can even conceive of finally completing the climb, for there is always likely to be a new terrain emerging. From this perspective, Martin Luther King's classic phrase that he had climbed the mountain and seen the promised land, is only relatively true; more than likely, the promised land was only a plateau from which new mountains would become visible as we approach them.

Equality As an Ultimate Goal

Yet, let me add that to recognize this chimerical characteristic of equality is not enough reason to forsake its pursuit. The goal itself is valuable because it provides a direction for deliberate change, and at the same time, a standard by which to assess the changes that do occur.

Societies are guided by human intentions and even by ideal goals, no matter how unattainable they may seem. These intentions have value in setting a tone and direction for societies. Who would now say, for instance, that the emancipation of the slaves in the U.S. was pointless simply because the American black today is still so far away from full social equality? Would it really have been better for us if we had not tried at all? Or, who would now agree with the Malthusian view that the poor deserve what they get, and because they may drag others down with them, they should not be helped to survive? Even the slightest progress to remedy the human condition is preferable to complete disregard or inaction. Tawney has phrased the choice very well.

It is true, indeed, that even such equality [of environment, circumstance, and opportunity], though the conditions on which it depends are largely within human control, will continue to elude us. The important thing, however, is not that it should be completely attained, but that it should be sincerely sought. What matters to the health of society is the objective towards which its face is set, and to suggest that it is immaterial in which direction it moves, because, whatever the direction, the goal must always elude it, is not scientific but irrational. It is like using the impossibility of absolute cleanliness as a pretext for rolling in a manure heap, or denying the importance of honesty because no one can be wholly honest. . . . And a society which is convinced that inequality is an evil need not be alarmed because the evil is one which cannot wholly be subdued. In recognizing the poison it will have armed itself with an antidote. It will have deprived inequality of its sting by stripping it of its esteem.[4]

Perhaps Tawney's conclusion that society is "armed with an antidote" by recognizing the evil of inequality is more optimistic than events would warrant. Certainly the racial violence in the U.S. in recent years is a case in which one would think that the antidote is about as deadly as the poison it is meant to neutralize. However, effective struggles to increase social equality are likely to be severe because the institutional structure of a society, almost inevitably, is under challenge. It is hard to conceive of any way by which economic and racial inequalities could be altered significantly without such challenges, given the reluctance and antipathy to change by those who have little to gain and much to lose. It is not that violent revolution is inescapable, but rather that, if institutions lose their flexiblity to make adjustments for needed remedies, then the likelihood of violence is increased and, in fact, can be justified by the search for equality. Remember that this view is an important part of our heritage as stated in the Declaration of Independence.

When in the Course of human events, it becomes necessary for one people to dissolve the political bands which have connected them with another, and to assume among the Powers of the earth, the separate and equal station to which the Laws of Nature and of Nature's God entitle them. . . . [T]hat whenever any Form of Government becomes destructure of these ends, it is the Right of the People to alter or to abolish it, and to institute new Government. . . .

The thrust of Tawney's argument is still sound today; the pursuit of equality is a major goal to which society dedicates its efforts, and this goal is still infinitely preferable to any opposing goal. Clearly, the very character of American society would be dramatically different were we either to abandon the goal of equality or to decide that the struggle just was no longer worth the effort. Similarly, American society would also be different were we to accept the conservative view that our accomplishments are good enough and that we can relax any further efforts. Few persons, I am convinced, would be prepared to forsake the struggle and to turn back history to an earlier system of rigid social distinctions frozen by law and by social practices. More persons, no doubt, would be prepared to stop where we now are. The consequences for our society, in both instances, would be disastrous as far as the values we now hold are concerned. As Tawney wrote, we should not roll in the dung heap simply because we know that absolute cleanliness is unattainable.

It should be made explicit that this stance toward equality—the straining toward what is unattainable—is far from an easy one to maintain. At the very least, it means the recognition of inevitable imperfections, and thereby, the companion recognition of the need to change as the situation demands. Everyone doubtless is "for" equality, but how many are "for" the tensions, insecurities, and social alterations that are associated with the search?

Consider how this latter condition can be developed into a rationale for accepting things as they are, and at the same time as a basis for accusing those who remain dissatisfied. In a review of Edward C. Banfield's book, *The Unheavenly City*,[5] sociologist Robert Nisbet strongly applauds the book for its central thesis that most, if not all, urban problems are as much the result of expectations rising faster than performances, as they are the result of real failures in American cities. Here a relevant passage from Nisbet's review can be quoted so that the underlying logic of his argument is made evident.

A new and seemingly unmanageable phenomenon is present in our society, one foreseen by [de] Tocqueville, one that, once created, feeds on itself. And this phenomenon is the dynamic tension provided by American middle-class *expectations*. . . . It was [de] Tocqueville who first put into systematic form the proposition that the greatest agonies over the problem of equality would be experienced precisely in those countries, such as the United States, where the work of equality has been carried the farthest, where substantive inequalities become even finer to the eye. . . . What he [Banfield] seems to be saying, in effect, is that urban problems, including poverty, schooling, medical service, housing, and employment income, in fact, the whole complex we call "urban crisis" is not likely to be dealt with in such a way as to remove present tensions and sense of impending conflict, for the reason that while affluence does indeed rise, *the sense of relative deprivation* rises also, and at a faster rate.[6]

Of course, the attempt to achieve equality is, in Nisbet's analogy, like trying to catch the mechanical rabbit at the dog track. Of course, there are tensions produced by the discrepancy between what one has been encouraged to expect and what one has been able to attain. However, the recognition that there are such states of tension does not automatically lend merit to Nisbet's position of looking backward at the distance we have come rather than looking forward to the distance yet to be covered. Indeed, we have enthusiastically embraced the Protestant Ethic with the inherent dissatisfactions and insecurities that it generates. I much prefer Tawney's view that every society needs a direction to follow, defined by what it believes to be the "good" and the "desirable." To stand still and to be satisfied with accomplishments to date is not enough; certainly it is not enough for those who cannot share in them.

This may appear to be an enslavement to the ideology of continued growth, which Nisbet has assailed in his other writings, but I see no option if the idea of equality is accepted and is meant to be effective. It makes little sense for those who continue to suffer from inequality to be content with general progress as long as their situation remains unaltered. Further, I believe that we seriously endanger the underlying structure and values of our own society by accepting a given level of attainment as the final stage. The reason for this view, simply stated, is that the definitions of equality necessarily must continue to change because of improved knowledge, greater experience, and continuously unfulfilled expectations. In other words, "relative deprivation" is not the undiluted social demon that Nisbet, Banfield, and others make it out to be. Instead, it is a social mechanism for change that we have accepted as part of our value system. If, in the future, values are discarded or significantly altered, then we will have started to become a vastly different kind of society than we now are.

EVALUATIONS OF EQUALITY

The fact that equality is a process, as I have stated, rather than an absolute condition implies that judgments about equality are always likely to be equivocal. This generalization holds true both for the assessment of the present situation as well as of the efforts being made to increase equality. Indeed, a major cause of current conflicts can be traced to the varying assessments that are made about where we are as a society and the speed of change we can allow. Hence, what to some is "all deliberate speed" toward greater equality, appears to others as no movement at all. What to some is a sincere desire to achieve greater equality, appears to others as just so much empty rhetoric.

The reasons for such differences come from the fact that the evaluation of equality versus inequality depends upon a number of separate elements, including (1) an assessment of the present situation compared with the past, (2) the knowledge of what contributes to inequality, and (3) a set of expectations regarding the future.

The first and last elements are fairly obvious. Hence, those who are satisfied with existing conditions tend to look backward and see the advances toward equality that have been made. By contrast, those who are dissatisfied look ahead and see only the gains that have yet to be made to improve existing conditions.

The second element, the knowledge about inequality, is less obvious but still crucial. Clearly, the toleration of inequality must depend upon the level of social knowledge of how society functions, of the values that are held, and of human behavior. We know more now than could have been known, say, 150 years ago. At that time, when it was accepted that the "poor are always with us" or that blacks are biologically inferior, then equality was meant to apply only to some persons. Consider, for example, that when Jefferson asserted in the Declaration of Independence that "all men are created equal," he could not have meant those words literally for there were wide variations in the social distinctions that already were evident in America. Some social mobility existed in the plantation-based aristocracies of the southern colonies, to take one example, but soon social distinctions became frozen and accepted as natural. As that brilliant analyst of the American South, W. J. Cash, noted:

Aristocracy in any real sense did not develop until . . . after 1700. From the foundations carefully built by his father and grandfather, a Carter, a Page, a Shirley began to tower decisively above the ruck of farmers, pyramided his holdings in land and slaves, squeezed out his smaller neighbors and relegated them to the remote Shenandoah, abandoned his story-and-a-half house for his new "hall," sent his sons to William and Mary and afterwards to the English universities or the law schools of London. These sons brought back the manners of the Georges and more-developed and subtle notions of class. And the sons of these in turn began to think of themselves as true aristocrats and to be accepted as such by those about them—to set themselves consciously to the elaboration and propagation of a tradition.[7]

Even in New England there were evident aristocratic social distinctions as Becker noted. "The rigid maintenance of class distinctions, even in New England, where students in Harvard College were seated according to social rank and John Adams was fourteenth in a class of twenty-four, made it presumptuous for the ordinary man to dispute the opinions of his betters or contest their right to leadership; to look up to his superiors and take his cue from them was regarded as the sufficient exercise of political liberty."[8]

The Relative Nature of Equality

Equality obviously did not mean absolute equality, but instead some kind of relative equality within a set of accepted limits. Indeed, T. V. Smith has contended that Americans kept searching for an argument by which they could establish their own definition of equality to replace the social inequalities imposed upon them by England. The Americans' purpose was to find reasons for their own special privilege as a just reward for having conquered a harsh environment and for having left the closed social system of the British. Therefore, they argued on whatever basis they could.

. . . first (1765) it is the "undoubted rights of Englishmen"; then (1774) not only the "principles of the English constitution and the several charters or compacts" but also the "immutable law of nature"; and, all this unavailing, the final appeal (1776) is to nature herself and to "certain inalienable rights." The motivation here is as clear as in Aristotle's celebrated advice to lawyers to "appeal to the law of nature" when the law of the land proves insufficient.[9]

Much more recently, the demands by blacks and other minority groups for admission into colleges and universities according to certain quotas regardless of admission standards, are reminiscent of the arguments just quoted. The substance differs, but the logic is very much the same. Where Jefferson appealed to the laws of nature, minority-group students today insist upon applying a law of society that inequality will be maintained until the circle is broken by open admissions.

The above comparison is intended to show that equality is not only a variable condition but also one that is forever tied to some set of standards which are temporary. Therefore, it is quite irrelevant to pursue a timeless definition which is absolute. Inasmuch as equality is a process and will change over time, so too will every definition that we wish to construct. What we might consider at this moment as "true equality" should not be carved into monumental marble, for it will soon become history and not continue as fact. We must expect that the future will produce new social understanding and that experience will dictate changes in these definitions. The only reason, in fact, that such a monumental phrase as "all men are created equal" can persist, is because its interpretation keeps changing even as the words remain the same. In this sense, all Americans behave like Supreme Court justices in supplying current meanings to hallowed phrases.

This shifting character of equality judgments, I must emphasize, results from an improved understanding of the way our society functions and of the social forces that create and maintain inequalities. Perhaps this is what makes it vital that we understand correctly the effects of any actions taken to correct inequality, lest those actions produce an opposite or unwanted result. We may move sincerely to redress certain social imbalances, but unless these actions are based on sound social understanding, the effect may well turn out to be the opposite of what was intended.

A Classical Inequity

That principle was well illustrated with regard to black voting rights. Blacks were systematically excluded from voting throughout the South by means of poll taxes and literacy requirements that were interpreted by white registrars. There is no question that these two requirements, plus physical threats against anyone who questioned them, served to deny large numbers of blacks the right to vote and was in direct violation of their constitutional rights. This situation changed, as was mentioned earlier, by the enactment of voting rights legislation in 1965. By this provision, federal voting examiners were sent into many sections of the South that had large black populations but very low black registrations. However, it would be foolish to contend that with voting restrictions removed and with larger numbers of blacks registered to vote, greater political equality has been achieved. The political structure and the exercise of political power, especially at the local level, are not altered overnight by raising black registrations.

In their assessment of the small gains made by southern blacks in the 1890s, Matthews and Prothro concluded that: "To give the franchise to an uneducated and impoverished minority in the face of vehement opposition from a united majority that controls the economic and social life of a region is likely to be fruitless—unless the minority is supported by force of arms from 'outside.' The vote alone—*without* other sources of power, *without* education or wealth or status, and *without* armed support—is not a sufficient resource for effective citizenship."[10]

After their studies of the effects of the 1965 voting law, Matthews and Prothro still concluded very much the same thing as they had for the earlier period. "This is not to argue that the vote is of little or no value to southern Negroes. It is to argue, however, that the concrete benefits to be derived from the franchise—under the conditions that prevail in the South—have often been exaggerated. To be sure, much of the extravagant talk about the vote being *the* key that will unlock the door to racial equality for southern Negroes should be discounted as political hyperbole."[11] One cannot dispute the force of this statement even though there have been marked gains since 1965 in the number of elected officeholders who are black. Important as it may appear (and I do not discount the enormous gains for improved treatment) to have a black sheriff, black councilmen, black school board members, and even a black mayor, this is still a long way from effective equality. Complex urban problems are no more easily solved by black than by white mayors. A recalcitrant white population can find other ways around the new political arrangements. It is not that such changes should be neglected but rather that we should look at them realistically for the consequences they can produce.

As in politics, so too in education, employment, and other areas of social life. It is at best naive and at worst dangerous to believe that these simple remedies will cure complex diseases. The search for equality is never easy, nor is it easy to correct social inequalities by isolated legal actions alone. Recent efforts in the areas of civil rights, educational desegregation, voting, and economic opportunities provide sufficient proof that the problems are complex and that judicial decisions, executive orders, and congressional acts are inadequate by themselves to achieve greater equality. Certainly, such actions are necessary because we are a society dependent upon laws, but, by themselves, such laws are insufficient to correct such wrongs. This is why more knowledge and understanding of social forces are critical if beliefs are to be translated into reality.

EQUAL OPPORTUNITIES AND MOBILITY

Some of the dilemmas and problems created by the search for equality have already been considered above—particularly the changing definitions of equality resulting from the improvement of social knowledge and changing social standards. Then, too, there was an explication of the dialectic character of such changes—changes by which social actions create reactions in a seemingly continuous chain. To these must be added a third element for consideration: the existence of equal opportunities for mobility by which equality can be implemented. Indeed, equality of opportunities always has been at the core of the American conception of equality, and the means by which these ideals were meant to be realized.

Past and Recent Views of Equality

In two brief sentences, de Tocqueville identified the essential meaning of equality for Americans. "Intellectual inequalities come directly from God, and man cannot prevent them from existing always. But it results . . . that, though mental endowments remain unequal as the Creator intended, the means of exercising them are equal."[12] De Tocqueville grasped the core of the American ideology, which does not assume equal talents but rather equal opportunities so that all persons might be able to develop according to their capabilities and endowments. His recognition expressed a dominant element of nineteenth-century liberalism that put primary emphasis upon the individual and made the state and society dependent upon a maximization of the individual's role. The idea was present also in Marx's dictum, "from each according to his ability, to each according to his need" even though Marx did not make the state and society secondary.

Lest one conclude that these beliefs are dated, let me quote from President Nixon's statement on desegregation in 1970. God is emphasized less by the President, but the rest of what he said could easily pass for an updated version of de Tocqueville.

Economic opportunity, education, social mobility—all of these, too, are essential elements of the open society. When we speak of equal opportunity we mean just that: that each person should have an equal chance at the starting line, and an equal chance to go just as high and as far as his talents and energies will take him. This Administration's program for helping the poor, for equal opportunity, for expanded opportunity, all have taken a significantly changed direction from those of previous years. . . . Instead of making a man's decision for him, we aim to give him both the right and ability to choose for himself—and the mobility to move upward.[13]

The crux of the problem, as phrased by de Tocqueville and President Nixon, is not whether we believe in upward social mobility, for this belief is as basic to our values as motherhood. Instead, it is whether social mobility is as much a possiblity as we would like to believe.

Mobility and Stratification

The problem is a critical one, for restricted access to available opportunities must lead to a state of reduced equality. If, for example, most individuals come to inherit these opportunities or lack of them for education, income, occupation, and general social position, then to that extent inequalities become established. In effect, their "talents and energies" have little to do with the position they get. If, by contrast, the effects of such inheritance are neutralized so that all individuals have "an equal chance at the starting line" as President Nixon put it, then inequality is simply a fair result of individual competition. It is the latter meaning that Americans attach to the equality ideal, and it is upon this meaning that Americans base their belief in equality. Therefore, the determination of social mobility is critical for an assessment of equality in American society today.

It is a fact of social existence that all societies are stratified. As was noted in the introductory chapter, the form of stratification and the values that are used to support it will vary from one society to the next, as well as from one time to another. Some form of stratification is inevitable, especially in developed societies such as ours in which numerous criteria for stratification are at hand. In its most general expression, stratification is the result of the fact that each society prizes some values above others. It may be military prowess, religious beliefs, or as in our society, scientific and entrepreneurial skills. Given this hierarchy of values, societies become organized so as to allocate their highest rewards and greatest prestige to those individuals who exhibit the prized talents. In this manner, individuals become located within social strata, theoretically at least, based upon the relevance of their talents and skills to the major social values of their society.

Of course, this is a highly stylized and mechanical view of stratification. It is very unlikely that such things work out so neatly in reality, especially in complex, industrial societies where a number of competing social forces are operative. Political and economic power, for instance, may be exercised not so much because a particular social stratum has the support of the value system for its endeavors, but because of the grip of individuals on the decision-making institutions. For example, black leadership has developed effective political strength built partly upon the guilt of white persons, just as white segregationists have developed their source of political strength built upon the fears of other white persons. In neither case does this power stem from a neat translation of some "contribution" to a major social value. In any case, and for many reasons, the system of social stratification necessarily comes to structure the social inequalities within a society.

Yet, following the reasoning of de Tocqueville and President Nixon, the fact of social stratification need not dampen one's confidence in the opportunities for equality, at least in theory. Presumably, all individuals should have equal access to opportunities so as to achieve upward mobility, wherever they may begin in the social hierarchy. This is why, in the face of manifest inequalities, Americans can believe that children born to poor parents can rise to become Nobel laureates, brilliant surgeons, wealthy industrialists, or great political leaders.

Even though we can think of shining exceptions, it has become apparent from our knowledge about societies that a system of social stratification tends to perpetuate the existing hierarchy simply by providing differential access to the channels for upward mobility. President Nixon's faith, expressed in the above quotation that "each person should have an equal chance at the starting line," is not justified by the logic of the way societies function in fact. Many sociologists have analyzed this phenomenon and have concluded that the old saw about the rich getting richer is substantially correct. For instance, Melvin Tumin has argued, "[T]he unequal distribution of rewards in one generation tends to result in the unequal distribution of motivation in the succeeding generation. . . . [Furthermore], there is some notice-able tendency for elites to restrict further access to their privileged positions, once they have sufficient power to enforce such restric-tions."[14]

It is not just cynicism that admits that children born of well-to-do parents, for example, do not begin from the same "starting line" as do the children born of poor parents. Even rich children, of course, can turn out to be failures, but they are penalized less, if at all, than are failures born to the poor. Furthermore, the allowable tolerance for failure is greater among the upper and middle classes than for those lower down in the class scale; the poor are not likely to have a second chance. Is there really any doubt about who is most likely to fare better: the son of a black rural family in Mississippi or the son of a white, urban, middle-class family in California? To be born poor in the U.S. in the early 1970s effectively means that the individual is very likely to stay poor his whole life. We really do not have regular channels to identify and reward so-called native talents and abilities in a systematic man-ner. The opportunities which were meant to be open to persons are, in fact, closed for a number of them, and these are likely to suffer failure as a result at every significant stage in their maturation and growth. What is more, these failures are cumulative, so that each failure increasingly lowers the probabilities of later success. We already know that this generalization holds true from the very start for those who receive an inferior or inadequate education. Also, we have learned recently that a shortage of proteins in the diet during the first two years of life, typical among the poor, causes significant brain and body damage that can never be corrected even by a proper diet in later years. The potential talents of the individual, thereby, can be effectively altered or destroyed even before he has had any chance to try to develop them. He is, in short, penalized from the moment of birth by his family situation.

Is Total Social Upheaval Unavoidable?

These social realities bring into sharp focus several critical elements that make the enforcement of equal opportunities very difficult, es-pecially if no deliberate steps are taken to equalize the situation: (1) As they mature, industrial societies function to create significant and lasting differences between the opportunities that are available to different strata in the population, (2) increased knowledge about how such societies function serves to make these differences more apparent to more people, and their basic beliefs about equality may be brought into question, and (3) as the knowledge about the systematic restriction of opportunities becomes part of the conventional "wisdom," the poten-tial conflict between older values and current realities becomes not only more likely but also possibly more severe. One must be very explicit about the underlying assumption of the above propositions:

The continued development of industrial society, as we know it, brings an increased rigidity to its system of stratification in the absence of deliberate and sustained efforts to the contrary.

These last observations logically raise another feature of equality that should be considered before going on to an analysis of social mobility. This feature has been called by Robin M. Williams, Jr., "equality of conditions."[15] In his analysis of equality in American society, Williams has noted " . . . that the principles of economic freedom and individual achievement have strongly dominated principles of equality. The reigning concept has been that of *equality of opportunity* rather than that of *equality of condition.* Concessions toward substantive equality of condition—for example, the income tax in so far as it is graduated—have not leveled differences in wealth; and the upper and middle classes of the society continually have insisted upon a moral claim to the existing differentials."[16] What this means is that substantive inequalities can be generated because (1) existing unequal conditions go beyond the legitimately justified or expected differences created by the competition for rewards and (2) that the conditions themselves interfere substantially with the realization of equal opportunities.

In the first instance, one could interpret Williams' observations to mean that the distribution of rewards in society is not justified by its accepted values. We may admit that the successful persons at the top deserve advantages that the failures at the bottom do not have. But, there are limits to the spread of those differences. This is why, for example, we wanted to prohibit aristocratic titles so as to prevent the creation of an elite which could establish its superiority in a formal way. Today, we can legitimately question whether it is reasonable for a few to own a great deal while many others suffer from malnutrition, and we can question whether sharp differences ought to exist in taxation, in due process, and in medical care. Certainly, we may accept the condition that some differences are going to exist as a result of differential rewards. Still, there are limits.

In spite of current rhetoric, I do not believe that this sort of questioning is at a revolutionary level in any real sense of that overused word. Yet, it is evident that in the demands of several minorities and of college students there appears the first sustained questioning of the legitimacy of these differences that we have had for quite some time. We have been made aware of an aspect of inequality that has been too often overlooked: that we cannot allow the differences between unequal strata—between classes—to increase without restriction. This judgment is precisely the matter at issue today as regards economic and racial inequalities. When the differences in conditions become grossly unequal, then it is necessary and reasonable to question whether such inequalities can be fully justified by our values. As Williams has noted, "It is perhaps especially crucial in a social system like that of the United States that differential rewards be apportioned both according to a *common set of standards of legitimacy* and to the *effective distribution of social power.*"[17]

PROBLEMS IN STUDYING MOBILITY—DEFINITIONAL AND METHODOLOGICAL

The second meaning of unequal conditions as mentioned above refers to the likelihood that the conditions under which individuals live also determine the range of opportunities open to them. It turns out, as will be shown in the following chapters, that the poor and the blacks must deal with inequality of opportunities as part of their unwanted heritage. This condition has been recognized, not only as expressed in the above quotation from President Nixon but also in the intent behind relevant federal legislation aimed at overcoming unwanted disadvantages. At least, this is how I read the efforts to improve schooling, to expand job training, and to increase employment opportunities for minorities. Whether these efforts can be successful is a matter to be left to a later analysis.

Definitional Problems

This latter meaning of *equal conditions* brings us back to a consideration of current trends of social mobility. Have opportunities for mobility increased or decreased in American society? Is stratification in America becoming more rigid or not? Clearly, if mobility is decreasing, then the maintenance of equal opportunities is also decreasing, and we can anticipate problems arising as a result of the inconsistency between values and realities. On the other hand, if mobility is still open, then to a degree so too are equal opportunities, and the task becomes one of balancing those opportunities, especially among the poor and the minority groups in American society.

The difficulty in trying to reach valid conclusions about the state of mobility in the U.S. is that there is rampant confusion about definitions, about the meaning of the statistics that are obtained, and about the validity of those statistics. Therefore, it is impossible to give a simple and unqualified answer to the questions that are posed. Yet, this is precisely the question that needs to be answered in order to evaluate the conditions of equality in the U.S. today and in order to estimate the severity of the problem in the near future.

The definitional problem of mobility is to identify precisely the levels between which mobility does or does not occur. In general terms, what we want to know is how feasible it is for people to rise out of one social class and into another. For example, what are the probabilities for those now in poverty to rise into the working class and to stay there? (It should be realized that, because the concept of "class" is itself open to several interpretations—as a status group, an occupational group, an income group, and a power group—any measure of social mobility between classes is similarly open to interpretation.) One who reads the reports and studies of mobility is justifiably confused because of the uncertainty about what is being measured. S. M. Miller once noted, "It has become common practice among sociologists to say 'social mobility' when we mean 'occupational mobility.' We become most readily aware of this tendency when we discuss 'social mobility' with nonsociologists who become concerned about our narrow usage of the term. . . . [S]ocial mobility is a multidimensional problem of which only one dimension is usually studied."[18]

Methodological Problems

As well as the definitional problem, we also must confront the problem of historical change, or in other words, the comparison between past and present rates of mobility regardless of how those rates are measured. Assuming that we know what we are measuring, how do we compare the differences between time periods so as to reach a valid conclusion about trends in mobility and opportunities for mobility? It is not enough, for instance, simply to compare the occupational distributions in two time periods, or as is usually done, to compare the occupations of sons with those of their fathers to see how much mobility has occurred between the generations. The reason is that the occupational structure itself changes over time so that the demand for particular occupations in one period is not likely to be the same in another period. This same type of change becomes even more difficult to measure when, instead of occupations or income, we try to consider such subtle dimensions as power or prestige.

It is not necessary to describe the other methodological problems that are involved in the analysis of social mobility, except to illustrate that there is room for confusion even when the data appear sound. For example, a study of occupational mobility in the U.S. by Peter M. Blau and Otis D. Duncan[19] represents the most detailed recent analysis of the subject. Even so, there are contradictory conclusions, apparently not intended by the analysts. After explaining that they could not give an answer directly to their question of "whether the working class has poorer chance of upward mobility than the middle class," the authors rephrased the question in occupational terms to ask whether "men who start careers in manual work are less likely than others to achieve an occupational status that differs from that of their fathers." Their answer is yes, although they insist on stating it in convoluted prose: "Men who begin their working lives in the working class, by contrast [with white-collar and farm workers] seem to have a less fortunate fate and end up in occupational positions that differ little from those of their fathers." This is to say, more simply, that if your father was a manual worker, the chances are that you will be too. Blau and Duncan, however, seemed to overlook some of these earlier and intricate conclusions in their later, more generalized statements: "The rates of upward mobility in the United States are still high. . . ." Or, "The stability of American democracy is undoubtedly related to the superior chances of upward mobility in this country. . . . " I do not claim to have combed the entire book for similar inconsistencies, but if these are representative, then I would conclude that the study of mobility and opportunity has some severe ideological problems in addition to the considerable methodological ones mentioned above.

Another factor affecting the interpretation of mobility is institutional change. For example, economic changes can radically alter the distribution of the labor force because new occupations will arise, older occupations may disappear, and the demand between occupations will fluctuate. It is easy to recall the change in the 1971 market for college graduates and even for graduates with advanced degrees. In the same way, there are also likely to be changes in income distribution, making an interpretation of comparative mobility a risky task. Because of those variations in occupational distributions, in income distributions, and in educational attainments, it is difficult to derive valid conclusions about mobility.

A final problem to be raised is the difference between objectively determined mobility on the one hand and, on the other, the subjective perceptions of the individual's opportunity for mobility. The issue is very relevant to the theme of this book. People act on the basis of their perceptions, which presumably bear some relationship to social reality. Problems can arise when individuals perceive a lack of opportunities for mobility, whether or not those opportunities exist in fact. By the same argument, as long as individuals perceive mobility as being available to them, they are less likely to challenge the existing structure and existing values. Unfortunately, we really have relatively little sound information as to how psychological perceptions relate to the character of social reality. In part, the confused nature of that reality as described above leaves us without any sound assessment; as a result, there may well be perceptual confusion. In part, too, people will perceive different parts of the mobility structure and thereby end up with different estimates as to its openness.

For example, a person who lives in poverty and is surrounded by poverty may likely perceive the opportunities that are open to him quite differently than a person who is in the working class. In the first instance, he may aspire to a steady job as the best move upward he could make. Others may have no aspirations at all, beaten or born into apathy and defeat. In a study I conducted in New Orleans in 1968, I sought to determine the aspirations held by a sample of poor people.[20] I found that the white poor were the least aspiring and least competitive of all class and race groups studied. The black poor, by contrast, expressed levels of aspiration that were both strong and realistic. Not only were they prepared to make the necessary sacrifices to achieve upward mobility, but also they were sensibly oriented toward moving into the working class rather than the more distant middle class.

In short, besides the changes in objective possibilities for upward mobility and equal opportunities, it is also necessary to consider the subjective perceptions concerning them.

THE VALUE OF MOBILITY

Beyond the methodological and definitional problems of social mobility and equality, there remains an overarching consideration of the value of such mobility for a society committed to attaining social equality. Here are two examples. The first is contained in an argument by Frank Parkin in his study of socialist societies. He contends that *downward mobility* may be a more critical index of the flexibility of the structure than is *upward mobility* as most American analysts currently assume.

There is some indication here that the Soviet educational system operates not so much to block upward mobility of lower status youths . . . but rather that it restricts downward mobility among the offspring of higher status groups. . . . S. M. Miller has suggested that rates of downward mobility are probably a better index of the openness of a class system than rates of upward mobility, and on this score the Soviet system, and that of other European socialist states, shows some signs of ossification. The opportunities for a lowly born child to improve his lot in socialist society by way of higher education are still considerably better than they are for his equivalent in capitalist society. But they are not quite so favourable as they were when the middle class was less integrated into the political and social order than it has now become.[21]

The second example is a value argument. Seymour Martin Lipset and Reinhard Bendix concluded, after their survey of the literature on social mobility, that the entire emphasis on mobility was misplaced anyway, particularly in the twentieth-century context of industrial societies.

The argument that increased social mobility will create a healthy society is part of the nineteenth-century intellectual tradition. Its rationale was strongest when the theory of increasing misery appeared most reasonable; that is, during the initial phases of the industrialization process, when it appeared to be true that "the rich got richer, and the poor got poorer." This theory appeared, and continues to be persuasive, in those societies in which the widening of opportunities produced by industrialization coincided with the amalgamation of aristocratic and newly rising bourgeois groups and hence with a stubborn retention of quasi-feudal privileges. . . . If it is true, as we have tried to show, that all developed industrial societies are characterized by a high rate of social mobility, it becomes questionable whether further studies of this phenomenon should be based on the implicit simple assumption that more mobility is a good thing.[22]

I could not disagree more with this contention because it assumes first that "a high rate of social mobility" already exists; and second, that the present rate—whatever it is—will remain unchanged in the future. As has already been described, there is enough confusion about the rates of mobility so as to make almost any firm conclusion about them suspect, including this one by Lipset and Bendix. However, they go further in their argument to contend that those who are not upward mobile have only themselves to blame.

Our findings also suggest that at the bottom of the social structure the problem is not merely one of "natural endowments" thwarted by inequality as has been assumed previously. Although so much attention has been given to the task of disentangling native intelligence and environmental influences that the problem of differences in motivation for achievement has become a subject for research only in recent years, the preliminary survey given above suggests that the cumulation of disadvantages at the bottom of the social scale is in large part the result of a lack of interest in educational and occupational achievement. In a country which is second to none in its concern with mobility and personal attainment it is clearly insufficient to attribute this lack of interest solely to the environment. Could it be that here is a built-in safeguard that enables those who have to shy away from the psychological burdens which mobility imposes?[23]

What a wondrously ingenious argument! What Lipset and Bendix have tried to do is to place the brunt of the fault upon unwilling individuals instead of upon the unyielding structure, by contending that inequality is primarily a psychological state rather than a social reality. It is, in fact, another way of stating Nisbet's contention, which is mentioned earlier: Inequality is not a structural phenomenon but the result of psychological interpretations and expectations—or lack of them in this case. If one takes this tack then *social* inequality disappears as a problem, to be replaced by a psychologically induced *personal* inequality, whatever that might mean. I could not disagree more, and the remainder of the book will show why.

As has been emphasized throughout this chapter, social inequality and social differences are to be expected. The crucial assessment to be made, however, is the extent to which equality or inequality of opportunities now prevails. As long as the social inequalities we encounter are produced by the differences of individual talents and motivations, and as long as the rewards are not blatantly unfair, then there is no serious attack upon the central value system because we would still be progressing toward the goal. However, when it becomes apparent (if it does) that social inequalities bear little relationship to differences in motivation, but instead, stem from differential opportunities for individuals by reason of race, sex, ethnicity, or family position, then the belief in equality is challenged, and the reality of inequality becomes more visible. My own studies do not support the conclusions that individual motivations are lacking in the case of the poor. At the very least, then, there is some basis to believe that motivations for success are still present, but that the system is not as open as it was thought to be.

Herein lies the real "American Dilemma." The issue is not simply one of believing in the "creed of equality" and acting in terms of inequality in the sense that Myrdal described. Rather, the issue is one of determining whether there is equality of opportunity or not—in other words, whether upward mobility is possible for those who pursue it. From this perspective, the study of mobility is never likely to become outdated or superfluous.

Having considered some of the problems in the way of studying inequality and the difficulties faced by a society that is dedicated to the pursuit of equality, let us consider in greater detail the specific conditions of the poor, and in a later chapter, the blacks in America today.

3
Poverty and Inequality

Social inequalities can generate problems for society because they raise doubts about the continued validity of the concept of equality. In the preceding chapters, a number of aspects of those problems have been discussed in a general way, and also, it has been shown that the mere existence of a discrepancy between belief and reality does not trigger social reactions automatically. The purpose now is to focus more closely upon two central manifestations of the discrepancy: poverty, to be discussed in this chapter, and race, to be discussed in the following chapter. In addition, there will be not only an analysis of the conflicting social forces that have been stimulated by the recognition of those inequalities but also an assessment of the likely direction of such forces in the future. The significant question underlying this analysis, then, is whether or not we can learn about the character of American society in view of the fact that our traditional belief in equality has now been publicly challenged by a national recognition of inequality.

RESISTANCE TO CHANGE

During the last two decades we have questioned the traditional view that racial and economic inequalities are inevitable but presumably temporary conditions for individuals who would overcome them. Considering the enormous amount of national effort and the resources that have been expended in trying to improve the situation of the poor, the blacks, and other minorities, it is reasonable to conclude that such inequalities have now assumed a new role in our national consciousness. It is not that we lacked poor people or escaped racial discrimination in earlier periods. Rather, the situation has come to be redefined so that we are no longer so convinced that inequalities will be automatically improved; such reasoning thus presents a possible challenge to our traditional values about equality.

My assessment of recent events is that Americans have altered their earlier view—a view that embodied almost unquestioned acceptance of equality as a real goal to which their society was formally dedicated. Whereas once that belief was an article of faith, we now have been forced to make some realistic adjustments, and thereby, to redefine that belief in important particulars. Our current problems, generated by poverty and race, have revealed strains upon the set of equalitarian values we have traditionally held. Hence, some have become convinced that equality ideals have been pushed further away from any possible realization, and that, without serious modifications in the institutions of American society, they will become little more than empty sentiments. Others have come to believe that the efforts spent in trying to remedy the inequalities of poverty and race are misplaced, that we have done more than enough, and that those people pretty much deserve what they get. The rhetoric of equality continues, but it has come to mean different things than it once did.

I make these observations without cynicism. I believe that the level of our understanding and knowledge has increased so that we are more aware, probably than ever before, of the difficulties and obstacles in the way of achieving equality. In short, we have learned that the belief in equality requires directed social change to refashion critical aspects of our institutions if that belief is to remain effective. We no longer can take for granted that our society will continue to change by itself and in a positive direction. Neither can we accept the view that quick and easy solutions are possible, whether advanced by revolutionaries or reactionaries. We are wiser now than before in the ways of social change, although perhaps still not wise enough in how to apply this wisdom.

We have moved well beyond the "dilemma" that Myrdal used to describe Americans almost thirty years ago, and into a condition where the complexities of inequality and the efforts to do something about them have almost overwhelmed us by their suddenness. Earlier perhaps, racial and economic discrimination could be tolerated, in spite of the moral dilemma it created, because we believed that inequality was more the result of personal failures than of institutionalized discrimination against a race or a class. We continued to depend upon history which proved that ghetto residents could escape if only they had the ambition to do so. Only recently, however, have we begun to understand that unequal opportunities have become a stable feature of American society, so that large numbers of Americans are condemned to remain in the ghettos less through their own fault and more through the fault of society.

Here, I must admit to cynicism in view of the lateness and the reluctance of so many persons to recognize the structural handicaps that poverty and race place upon individuals. If the "dilemma" exists today, then it is in the form of an ambivalence between an emotional need to believe in equality and a reluctance to recognize the depth of inequality and to do something about it. Furthermore, the ambivalence probably is highest among those persons who feel that they have something to lose by any serious attempt to correct inequalities. Those in the working class, for example, may feel both jealous and insecure with their status. To do something about inequalities of poverty and race means, among other things, a threat to the working-class person's position by giving others the advantages that he did not have and also by questioning the effort he has made to attain and to keep his position. The same is becoming true for those in the middle class as well because their hard-won advantages are given more easily to others, as in the case of open college admissions or financial aid to students from low-income groups. Sooner or later, most individuals are likely to be affected in a similar manner.

Unfortunately, we do not know how widespread or potent is this kind of class insecurity. However, let me propose an interpretation, using some recent information on the changes in class identification over the past decade. According to a summary report of several studies by the Survey Research Center at the University of Michigan, Schreiber and Nygreen[1] found that 46 percent of employed men in 1958 identified themselves as "working-class," while in 1968, 34 percent made the same identification. What is particularly relevant is the variation over the period among men in different occupations who identified themselves as "working class." Hence, in 1958, 27 percent of those who were in the professions, business, and white-collar jobs said that they were "working-class." The percentage was almost the same (21 percent) ten years later. Among those in manual work, by contrast, 63 percent identified with the working class in 1958, but ten years later the proportion dropped markedly to 47 percent. This shift I see as a clue to the present mentality of manual workers, conceivably tense about their social position. Specifically, it can be suggested that the shift by one-quarter of this group to an identification with higher prestige classes above the working class means a consciousness of a new status or at least an expression of this intent. Furthermore, it is possible that these are the very individuals who are reluctant to endanger this status by opening opportunities to the poor. To be sure, this is a heavy weight of interpretation to place upon a solitary statistical fragment, but when added to the visible reactions by segments of the working class—reactions against increased welfare and measures to lessen job discrimination—then perhaps this interpretation is somewhat more valid.

In any case, the recognition by the larger society of existing inequalities is less in doubt, as measured by the countless programs aimed at trying to redress racial and economic imbalances.

Awareness is one thing; effective remedies, however, are quite another. If that assumption is correct, then existing institutions must be changed significantly if there is to be any gain in overcoming inequalities. Inequalities no longer can be dismissed or discounted as temporary conditions that automatically will be improved. Either institutional change occurs or we probably have reached a point where our traditional belief in both equality and opportunity itself must be changed. I am not persuaded that, as a society, we have to admit to existing inequalities as we did about twenty years ago. Nevertheless, having recognized them and having formally admitted that they do exist, we now cannot simply forget the whole thing and turn back the clock. The recognition, the programs of assistance, and the resultant correction were significant institutional changes themselves—changes that now must be developed until some new stability is achieved. For instance, to have stated that unequal opportunities exist or that inferior schooling creates a lasting social inferiority is to have brought some of our most cherished assumptions under scrutiny. We cannot now simply dismiss the entire matter; rather, we must somehow come to terms with it.

Here lies a major source of the problems we have been experiencing with inequality: Neither the conditions nor the values are easily changed. Whereas the American majority seeks to retain the value of equality with only minimal interference, the minority, being in its circumstances and being gripped by inequality, cannot always believe in the traditional value or be patient with the pace of change. The consequences of this condition are readily apparent in the actions of black militants. They are much less apparent among the poor, who are unorganized. I agree with Warren C. Haggstrom who has said that "it appears doubtful that the poor in the United States can secure an effective power base from which to organize to transform their relationships with the affluent society. . . . No matter how one counts them, the poor are a minority in the United States . . . [and] lack connections with the levers of power."[2] Still, the poor are a potential political constituency that could become militant if their situation remains unchanged and if leadership develops to mobilize them. This has happened before in history, and we should not automatically discount the possibility of its happening again.

The purpose in this chapter is to consider poverty and the poor. The overall attempt represents a means of analyzing a major aspect of America's class structure in order to learn whether or not inequality has now become a permanent feature of that structure. Although we find it impossible to reach valid conclusions about general social mobility (as was noted in the preceding chapter), one can attempt to illustrate such answers in a more specific analysis of the poor. Indeed, it is at the poverty level that mobility and inequality show significant interrelatedness; for if the poor cannot rise, then inequality is well on the way to becoming a permanent feature of American society.

PERSPECTIVES ON POVERTY

Within the last few years a small library of books and articles has been published on the subject of poverty. The titles cover a variety of topics that include historical, physiological, economic, psychological, political, and sociological studies as well as evaluations of poverty remedies and programs. No one can even pretend to cover this considerable literature faithfully and fully, any more than one who is not the rare history specialist could cover the literature on the American Civil War. On the other hand, there is really little purpose in trying to encompass the entire inventory when the immediate aim is one of understanding rather than one of attempting to compose a bibliography.

In order to move toward the objective of understanding poverty as a problem of inequality, much of the relevant literature on poverty is presented in three perspectives that serve to highlight the different views of poverty as a "problem" and of the quality of possible remedies. Not surprisingly, it will be shown that the "problem" of poverty depends very much upon the perspective that is taken, and that the remedy in turn depends on the way that the "problem" has been defined.

The three viewpoints are these: (1) poverty as income, (2) poverty as culture, and (3) poverty as class.

Poverty As Income

By this first perspective, poverty is simply a category of persons to be defined and measured, and most obviously, to be measured in terms of income. This sounds like the easiest and most defensible definition to follow, for, as everyone ought to know, to be poor means to have very little or no money. What could be more obvious? As will be shown below, however, the obvious has ambiguities and problems of its own, so that we end up more confused and uncertain than we would be by using some seemingly more complicated definition.

One of the most frequently used measures of poverty was one established by the Social Security Administration. It incorporates a poverty level that is variable, reflecting cost-of-living increases. For a nonfarm family of four in 1969, the poverty line was $3,743, and as in previous years, was a figure based "on the minimum food and other needs of families, taking into account of family size, number of children, and farm-nonfarm residence."[3] In 1969, there were 24.3 million Americans classified as poor by this definition, "a decrease of 1.1 million since 1968 and 15.2 million over the past decade."[4] As will be shown shortly, such appreciable improvements need to be surrounded with a considerable number of qualified statements and reservations.

As is the case with many interpretations based upon statistics, this one also has strengths and weaknesses stemming from its arbitrariness. Its strength is that it can be applied toward a clear, objective definition of poverty that can be measured and thereby traced over a period of time. Its weakness is that the definition of income level requires social interpretations that are necessarily variable. Different interpretations are invited by a phrase such as "minimum food and other needs of families"—a standard used in the income definition of poverty. Indeed, what is such an income, and how valid is it to imply the use of a double standard, one for the poor and one for those who can afford better? The point has been made, by foes and friends of poverty programs alike, that the American poor probably are better off economically than most people in developing and economically depressed countries such as India, Tanzania, or Guatemala. However, the international comparison is much less relevant than the one between the poor and the affluent in America itself, where the differences are visible and evident. In this case, what is an "acceptable" minimum income needed to live, not just survive, in America?

At best, an income definition of poverty is a convenient yardstick for distinguishing rather gross changes in the numbers of poor. Even so, this type of information should not be accepted blindly. For example, in 1969 we were informed that, "Between 1959 and 1968 the number of poor persons in the United States declined from 39 million to 25 million."[5] However, such a game of numbers raises justifiable suspicions when this latter estimate is compared with one made a year earlier.

In 1966 the poverty line for a nonfarm family of four was $3,335, however according to the most recent BLS [Bureau of Labor Statistics] expenditure survey, it would require an income of $9,200 for a family of four to achieve a modest but adequate standard of living in most of our large cities. In 1959, the poverty line for families of this type was $3,100 while a modest but adequate budget cost approximately $7,000 (in 1966 dollars). Thus, the poverty line, as determined by official criteria, *has not maintained its earlier relationship to the modest but adequate level of living for U.S. urban families.*[6] [Emphasis added.]

The point is that income definitions alone are always relative; poverty income levels always will fluctuate as we search for a current definition either of the "modest but adequate level of living" or of the "minimum food and other needs of families." Such definitions are also relative in another sense. Community standards and individual expectations change, and so too must the income level in order to reflect them. There are, as Edward Banfield has noted, feelings of "relative deprivation" among the poor. "The poor today are not 'objectively' any more deprived relative to the nonpoor than they were a decade ago. Few will doubt, however, that they *feel* more deprived—that they perceive the gap to be wider and that, this being the case, it *is* wider in the sense that matters most."[7] Banfield relies on this interpretation to argue that little can be done, therefore, to erase poverty because feelings of relative deprivation will forever outpace any material improvement. I am not at all convinced by Banfield's conclusion, even though the initial observation on which it is based is substantially correct. I would have thought that such feelings of relative deprivation were part of the bedrock on which our expanding economy has traditionally been based, and it is illogical to blame the poor for insisting upon sharing this value.

We must conclude, therefore, that the initial convenience of an income measure to define poverty is restricted both in its timeliness and, especially, in its interpretation. The income definition can be adequate for some immediate and limited purposes, but in its application and interpretation we need to be quite cautious.

Perhaps the most severe error has been to pursue income definitions of poverty in the mistaken belief that somewhere a solid answer can be found—an error that is only dreadfully compounded by basing policy on the outcome. It is evident that this view of poverty has wide appeal, especially for policymakers. Given an income line to separate the population, the objective clearly becomes one of trying to move people and families above the poverty line by some sort of pure income supplement such as a negative income tax or an incentive welfare program. All such devices are aimed at putting more money into the hands of poor families and thereby decreasing their numbers according to whatever is the current income definition of poverty. Unfortunately, we are lulled into believing that the problem of poverty gets solved by this kind of simple tampering with incomes.

Yet, some will object to my conclusion on the grounds that the path to the solution of poverty must be reached by getting more money into the hands of the poor. My response to this view is that its proponents usually interpret income in such a limited fashion that their "solution" to the problem is hardly a "solution" at all. For one thing, unless increased economic opportunities are provided along with the increased income, there is likely to be very little effective change in the situation for the poor. Added income does little more to solve problems than do current welfare payments.

Second, unless there is more widely effective access for social participation, then income alone cannot help to remedy even the economic consequences of poverty. To quote from the President's Commission on Income Maintenance Programs:

[I]f it is true that poverty in America excludes its victims from the ongoing social order, an acceptable living standard will require not only the minimum food, shelter, clothing, and physical health—generally covered by "poverty budgets"—but also the means to achieve social participation and a full development of individual talents. Individual fulfillment and satisfying involvement in the larger society requires not just a command of goods and services for comfortable consumption levels, but also for individual investment in education, training, recreation, etc. Only when these investment objectives are added to the definition of poverty can the community make real progress in eliminating poverty, instead of just temporarily alleviating its symptoms.[8]

Finally, unless income differences are interpreted as signs of the larger condition of inequality, then the minor tampering with strictly income solutions misses the need for a significant form of income redistribution that could be more lasting. S. M. Miller and Pamela Roby,[9] following this line, have suggested alternatives that contrast quite sharply with the more simple income view. They identify a *comparative-income* approach and an *income-share* approach that they see as preferable. In the first, they suggest that the median or mean family income be taken as the standard and that the poverty line be drawn at 50 percent of that standard. "This approach," they write, "openly embraces the notion that the condition of poverty is an inequality phenomenon—the poor are those who have fallen behind the grades and standards of the society as a whole. . . . "[10] In the income-share approach, they suggest that poverty be defined by the share of the total national income that is received by the bottom 10, 20, or 30 percent of the population. "In this approach," they argue, "poverty is sharply regarded as inequality. It is the income fate of a specific group which is at the bottom of the society that is the issue. Obviously, from this perspective, we cannot have trends in the number and percentage of the poor. The question instead is: How well is the bottom group doing?"[11] Contrast, if you will, this conception with the one advanced by Banfield and quoted previously. Banfield has presented the concept that the poor keep wanting more, just as everyone else does; Miller and Roby imply that, instead of trying to discourage the poor from that view, we should be building upon it to improve their situation.

My objection to the income definition of poverty, then, is that it takes a very narrow view of income and does not include the functions of income that we normally accept: (1) freedom of choice in its use, (2) a means to enhance effective participation in one's community, (3) a means to increase economic opportunities, and (4) a means to have greater control over one's life. One could go further and contend that the usual discussions of income as an antipoverty measure tend to conceal an implicit ideology that "there should be superimposed, upon the poors' freedom of choice, behavior patterns that are satisfying to the nonpoor."[12] The absence of discussion of these dimensions in current income programs is an indication of the welfare ideology as expressed in the last quotation. Unless income solutions, therefore, are tied to an explicit recognition of the concept of poverty as economic inequality in the sense suggested above, I fear that programs for income assistance will solve little, if anything, of the poverty problem.

Poverty As Culture

If the income perspective of poverty appeals to policymakers and economists because of its supposed simplicity, then the perspective of poverty as culture appeals to a broad spectrum of social scientists because it fits their disciplinary biases. Briefly stated, by the cultural view, poverty is seen as "a subculture of Western society with its own structure and rationale, a way of life handed down from generation to generation along family lines . . . a culture in the traditional anthropological sense that it provides human beings with a design for living, with a ready-made set of solutions for human problems."[13] Particularly for sociologists and anthropologists the perspective is comfortable because it is conceptually familiar in that it identifies a segment of society in terms of its values, beliefs, and practices.

The poor, and at times the lower class generally, are characterized as members of a distinct cultural group, separated somehow from the main cultural forces of the national society. This "subculture" may be seen either in positive or negative terms, but in both cases the effect is to distinguish the poor as culturally different. Negatively, the poverty culture is viewed as "pathological" in that "it constitutes a disorganized, pathological, or incomplete version of major aspects of middle-class culture."[14]

The positive view, which has gained rather general acceptance among social scientists, sees this culture as a functionally adequate adjustment to the conditions of poverty; as with any culture, it too serves to make the environment viable for those who must live in it. For instance, this is the tack that Lee Rainwater has taken using the sociological concept of function. The lower class, he argues, exists as a subculture in the midst of the larger culture but yet distinct from it because it must devise its own norms and means for adjustment.

This functional autonomy of the lower-class subculture is in the interest of both the larger society and of the lower class. The lower class requires breathing room free from the oppressive eye of conventional society and, therefore, from the oppressive application of conventional norms. Conventional society is freed from the necessity to confront the fact that the norms are constantly flaunted and that the social control mechanisms that are supposed to insure observance cannot operate effectively.[15]

There are many objections to that characterization, not the least of which is the assumption that cultures are fully rational in their responses to some specific need. Further, the same description could be applied to any so-called deviant subculture (criminals, drug addicts, etc.) and make as much sense, which is to say that nothing is really explained. Finally, if isolation of the lower class really does exist and happens to be functional, then any deviation from a norm could be isolated and made to appear functional in the same way. What, then, does it take to challenge and to substantively alter the general norms when conflicts and dysfunctions are encountered? Or do the general norms simply remain unchanged by allowing subcultural deviations to create their own special environment? There seems to be no answer to these questions in Rainwater's formulation. However, that is not so unusual because it is also a general criticism to be directed against most of the subcultural descriptions of poverty.

A not-so-implicit assumption of the cultural perspective is that the poor can and must live within a culture that is distinctively different from the larger culture. There is an attached implication in this view that little can be done (or for some, even should be done) to try to change this situation. Charles Valentine, whose critical analysis is acute and perceptive, has reached a conclusion with which I strongly agree.

My own view of this model [the culture of poverty] is that the main weight and prevailing direction of available evidence are inconsistent with it, even though most of those reporting the evidence seem to be more or less committed to this interpretation. When it is presented as a total picture of the culture of the lower class, in my considered judgment this portrayal is absurd. In this form it is little more than a middle-class intellectual rationale for blaming poverty on the poor and thus avoiding recognition of the need for radical change in our society.[16]

In spite of the criticisms that, at the very least, raise some doubts about the bias of cultural interpretations, much of the current social-scientific wisdom favors this view of poverty. Even in the face of considerable evidence to the contrary, social scientists writing in this subject area seem to be unwilling to reconsider their bias. Moreover, Rossi and Blum systematically screened every issue of the major sociological journals from 1950 to 1966 in order to determine whether the empirical evidence pointed to poverty as a difference in *degree* rather than in *kind* from other social strata. Their conclusions were unequivocal.

There is little firm evidence for the existence of a "culture of poverty" which marks off the very poor as distinctively different from SES levels [socioeconomic status] immediately above them. The poor appear to be quantitatively rather than qualitatively different.[17]

To separate poverty from the American mainstream as a distinct subculture tends either to avoid the question of equality and inequality or to make the issue meaningless. In fact, that view comes to isolate the poor entirely by the presumption of cultural relativism—in other words, that cultures cannot be evaluated in comparison with one another. Hence, the question of whether equality is enhanced by one culture as compared with another becomes irrelevant within such a framework. Just as it would be considered nonsense to ask whether the Ashanti are culturally equal to the Swiss, so too, the poor are defined only as different (not "better" or "worse") from those who are not poor. There may be some justification for this stance when it comes to comparing national cultures, but there is hardly any justification when it comes to comparing groups within a single culture.

It also follows from the cultural view that action to correct the situation of poverty clearly is irrelevant because one does not change cultures; one only observes them. In every other view of poverty there is at least some room for believing that poverty might be overcome either through some affirmative action or by self-correcting mechanisms within the society. Here, however, there is a commitment to the view that the poor have adjusted to their cultural environment and that there they will remain. And, as with all cultures, succeeding generations are socialized into the same established pattern of their parents. What an easy solution to the problem of inequality.

It may appear that the discussion has been directed more toward remedies than toward theories and perspectives. Of course, the two can be separated and considered independently. However, in this case there is an intimacy between theory and application that cannot be dismissed. For one thing, the extension of theories about poverty to include so-called "practical" consequences can illuminate some of the conceptual faults in the theories themselves. As has been shown, a consequence of the cultural perspective is to do nothing about the poor because one should not tamper with another group's culture. But, the weakness of the perspective is its assumption that, in relation to the larger culture, a subculture of poverty somehow is independent with regard to the matter of inequality. In the light of this previous statement, the subcultural view needs to explain how the subculture survives as a contradiction of a major social value. How can the view avoid the appearance of being dysfunctional when seen from the perspective of the larger cultural system?

For another thing, theories about poverty have practical consequences whether the theorists are aware of them or not. Just as the publication by a reputable scientist that blacks are genetically inferior in intelligence to whites provides material for political purposes, so too the publication by scientists of their view of poverty generates possible political consequences. A number of articles and discussions about the causes of poverty have affected policy decisions or otherwise helped to shape the public's views. Such consequences are unavoidable costs that the poverty theorists must recognize, and the pleading of deliberate ignorance on this score is no excuse. A telling argument on the relationship between theory and application has been made by William Ryan, who has faulted scientists and others for not perceiving their biases in the way they view current social problems.

Perhaps the most fundamental question to ask of those who are enamored of the idea that the poor have one culture and the rich another is to ask, simply, "So What?" . . . The effect of tastes, childrearing practices, speech patterns, reading habits, and other cultural factors is relatively small in comparison to the effect of wealth and affluence. What I am trying to suggest is that the inclusion in the analytic process of the elements of social stratification that are usually omitted—particularly economic class and power—would produce more significant insights into the circumstances of the poor and the pressures and deprivations with which they live. . . . The need to avoid facing this obvious solution [a substantial redistribution of income] . . . provides the motivation for developing the stabilizing ideology of the culture of poverty which acts to sustain the status quo and delay change. The function of the ideology of lower class culture, then, is plainly to maintain inequality in American life.[18]

Perhaps this argument has been extended to a point that is unjustified, since the proponents of the cultural perspective could contend that poverty might be altered by means of directed cultural changes. In other words, they suggest that the poor could be deliberately and systematically inducted into the American middle-class culture by "social work, psychiatry, and education," as Valentine has put it.[19]

But, I am not very sanguine about the probabilities for success of directed cultural change. For one thing, we just do not know enough about the numerous and complex interrelationships between cultural elements so as to control or predict the direction of such change. For another, even if we did, I doubt that there would be much effective power behind decisions that would require such a threatening impact upon existing social institutions. Some may think it is feasible to try to get the poor to embrace middle-class values such as a desire for upward mobility, saving, and deferred gratification. This is hardly an adequate solution, however, unless the conditions producing economic inequalities are not changed at the same time. What is the point of teaching the poor to behave like the middle class unless there are substantial and simultaneous changes in their employment, education, housing, and the like? Here is where the cultural view simply falls apart because it assumes, in large measure, that poverty is primarily a consequence of a special type of socialization—the fault of the poor themselves. If we were to change those values without changing the actual situation, though, would we really have made any progress? I believe not, for inequality and unequal conditions are at the root of the problem, not simply the values held by the poor themselves.

Poverty As Class

My major criticism of the income and cultural views of poverty is that, whatever substance they may add to the understanding of the subject, they avoid any significant characterization of poverty as a manifestation of inequality, which I believe is its most elementary meaning. Even by the income perspective, which presumably could have some merit in the consideration of inequality, poverty emerges as a narrow problem involving income—a view that misses the significance of income as a means for making effective economic choices or for opening up access to further economic opportunities. It is impossible to escape the conclusion that those who propound this view are aiming for little more than minimal income supplements which are meant, at best, to bring the poor just above the subsistence level. What is more, even if this approach were successful, it is doubtful how long it would be effective. By the cultural perspective, the poor are treated as culturally isolated and distinct from the mainstream of American society. Rather than assessing this condition as a commentary on possibly unequal standards within our society, the argument for the cultural perspective moves only toward an assessment of the culture of poverty as a satisfactory adjustment for the poor. The only reasonable conclusion I find here is that the poor somehow must be qualitatively different, as though belonging to an alien and foreign society.

One can juxtapose to the above two perspectives a third, by which poverty is defined as a phenomenon of class, and thereby, as an inescapable feature of social inequality. The poor belong to the lowest social stratum of the American class structure. They lack any effective access to social, political, and economic institutions—a situation which makes the poor virtually powerless to challenge or to control their environment. This condition is further compounded by the inability of the poor to organize themselves into a coherent and conscious class that might pursue power. In addition, it is quite likely that the poor judge themselves by the current standards of the society at large as failures or the victims of bad luck. (It can be noted here that this negative self-concept has been changed for many of the poor who are black, as a result of organization and the development of positive racial pride.) Far from being outside of the national mainstream, as the cultural proponents would have it, the poor as a class are very much a part of it. Their present class position is the result of the changes that have taken place in American society, just as their future is tied to whatever changes will occur.

As is the case with any class, the lower class can be distinguished by two features: (1) the conditions of existence, and (2) the situation that establishes the extent of access to society's rewards and benefits. The first can include all of those material features by which we identify differences among classes, as well as the standards typically associated with each class. Hence, the poor are easily distinguished from other classes by their housing, diet, education, economic goods, occupation, and employment. Without belaboring the obvious, the poor stand out by their lack of the goods and the access to services that we take for granted in an affluent society. Indeed, their lack is so apparent that it is surprising that we overlooked it for years until poverty was finally "discovered." With the second characteristic mentioned above, there is reference to the degree of control that the different classes can exert upon their social environment, which in turn is determined by the power typically held by the members in each class to shape social, political, and economic institutions. Such power, not surprisingly, is distributed in direct relation to the position of the class in the class structure, so that the upper class can command the most power and the lower class the least power over most of the available rewards and resources. For instance, whereas those in the upper class are able to lobby for legislation in their own behalf, or directly to affect political careers, or to gain economic concessions or to have the easiest access to good medical care, education, and housing, the poor are powerless on all of these grounds. They remain very much in the position of simply having to accept whatever filters down to them.

In spite of the fact that this situation has been described as though classes were coherent and organized entities, this is not fully the case. American society is not at the stage of having a tight class structure that is either fixed or fully articulated. For one thing, there is evidence of some social mobility in the middle ranges of the class structure, although some might argue that this movement is relatively insignificant. For another, Americans do not perceive of classes as being so organized that there is some consensus about the distinctions between those classes. Hence, classes in America are not viewed with the clarity that they are viewed, for instance, in England. Even so, there is plentiful proof that class does make a difference in the U.S. It explains a wide range of differences in behavior and conditions, including differences in physical and mental health, fertility, personality, and a number of attitudes.

Much of the haziness and equivocation about class and the consequences of class—ambiguities that exist when we try to describe the full range of the class structure—disappear when we concentrate upon the poor alone. There are disagreements, for example, over the standard used to separate the working class from the lower middle class, and indeed here, the general reluctance of Americans to think in class terms makes it difficult to determine precisely where the dividing line between those classes should be placed.* Much less difficulty, however, is encountered in the simpler separation of those at the bottom from others. As I have said, the poor are virtually powerless to control any aspect of their environment, and, as members of the lowest class, have almost no choices to make. They are, I believe, fixed in their positions with little, if any, opportunities for escape.

The nature of their inequality is evident on both elements identified above—the inequality of their conditions and the inequality of their access to opportunities. Obviously, such estimates of inequality are relative, depending upon comparisons with other classes. But the main point is that inequalities do raise serious questions about the equity that is present in the American system. The conventional response to this doubt about our central value system is to contend that the poor are not a manifestation of inequalities; either they deserve their fate as failures surely must, or the conditions of poverty are temporary so that, in the long run, those who are able and talented will rise above this class.

Unfortunately, neither of these rationalizations is quite accurate today. Many Americans probably would maintain that there have always been poor people in the United States, and that poverty is only a temporary condition for those with the ambition and desire to work hard and to get ahead. I believe that this judgment is unrealistic today, and therefore, is a tragic assumption because it justifies a lack of action to correct the problem. Poverty in an earlier period of our history was much less likely to be so fixed and permanent a condition for individuals as it is today, if only because the shape of our economic, political,

---

*Still, it may come as a surprise to learn that on a subjective basis, Americans have been rather steady in their class identifications. Studies by the Survey Research Center, based on nationwide samples for the years indicated, have shown close similarities in such identifications. These data do not contradict the point made earlier about a shift in the class identification of manual workers. The essential concept here is that even with possible shifts between classes, the overall proportions by class remain almost the same.

TABLE 3-1. **COMPARATIVE SOCIAL CLASS IDENTIFICATION, 1956 AND 1968**

Class Identification	1956	1968
Upper middle	6%	11%
Middle	33%	34%
Upper working	11%	11%
Working	47%	41%
Don't know	1%	2%
Reject class idea	2%	1%

Adapted from E. M. Schreiber and G. T. Nygreen, "Subjective Social Class in America: 1945–1968," *Social Forces*, 48 (March 1970), Table 1, p. 351.

and social institutions is different. At the time of the great waves of foreign immigration into the United States, around the turn of this century, there was fluidity within our institutional structure because we were developing as a nation and as an economy. The economy was characterized by an openness for upward mobility, as proven by the great numbers of those who moved from lower-class, immigrant origins into the more comfortable circumstances of the working classes or especially, the middle classes. Hard and fast status differences were difficult to establish because there was no long tradition of status upon which to build. Generally, there were no glorious and esteemed ancestors whose superior status could be conferred directly on descendants. Even access to the political mechanisms was relatively open, partly because of the enormous influx of new citizens into the polity, and partly because political organizations were directly dependent upon citizens at the lowest political levels. In brief, poverty in the earlier era could be temporary for large numbers because the economy was expanding, and numerous channels for control were relatively open. The mistake is to believe that all of this has not changed.

With each of the characteristics just mentioned, the conditions today are different because escape from the bottom of the class structure is closed. It is not necessary to embark on the highly complex and controversial discussion of who holds power in American society, but it should be pointed out that the opportunities for the poor today to rise and to succeed are less available and thereby more unequal than they once were. The economy today is more complex and more dependent upon technology than it once was. Upward mobility depends heavily upon more education, greater sacrifices of resources by individuals to pursue it, and a willingness to endure difficulties without assurances of success. Nor is it only a matter of education as a prerequisite for upward mobility. Education symbolizes the enormous differences in the height of the barriers that confront the poor today compared with that faced by the poor more than fifty years ago. The educational penalties that the poor must accept, from poor facilities to poor teachers, symbolize the unequal burdens for the poor as compared with other classes. The same patterns can be traced also in all other sectors of American society.

Related to these assessments is also the recognition that, as compared with an earlier period, the conditions of poverty diverge more markedly from the conditions experienced by other classes. In other words, the differences in the very style of life between rich and poor are greater and sharper today than before. Such differences, of course, are themselves a reflection of the changes in the economy toward more consumer goods and more services. Usually, that trend is cited as evidence of economic development and superiority brought about by an advanced technology and an advanced economic organization. Our widespread affluence, for instance, is portrayed in such positive terms. Yet, at the same time, the expansion of economic development also has functioned to increase the material differences between the poor and others. There is no question that wealthy families in an earlier era lived in a style that was markedly superior to other families. One of the highly sought benefits of our technology, however, has been the production of many goods and services at a price and in quantities that made them available to many others, not just the wealthy. That production has made it virtually impossible for the wealthy to monopolize economic goods and services for status reasons. Even working-class families, we pridefully maintain, are able to purchase a wide range of goods that once were priced outside of their budget. By contrast today, the poor are even worse off, and they are excluded from those benefits even as they are more widely accessible to others. This inequality of conditions is plainly evident in material goods, and it is also painfully evident in other spheres such as medical care, educational quality, and in the quality of justice that is dispensed. Being powerless, the poor cannot do very much to equalize conditions effectively, and it is quite likely that their situation continues to diverge more and more from the norms that apply to other classes. Thus, more than ever before, we have exacerbated the inequality of conditions that apply to the poor.

The significance of the class perspective, as well as of the changes that have affected the class structure, has been missed by many Americans, including a number of social scientists. Clearly, the income and cultural views lead to consequences for action that are much less severe than are those from the class perspective. I agree with Miller and Roby who have observed, "Poverty has become the acceptable way of discussing the more disturbing issue of inequality. Poverty has not been fully recognized as the shorthand for the much broader idea [of inequality] because the historic subsistence connotations of the term still survive. As a result, we have heated debates that fail to clarify issues or touch the real problems of the poor."[20]

The appeal of the income and cultural views appears to be that they require no serious assessment of American institutions and values. Whether one adopts the income view that a little money can be made to go a long way, or the cultural view that the poor have made a functional adjustment, the fault of poverty seems to remain squarely upon the shoulders of the poor themselves. At best, they might be given some help to get above the subsistence level or be taught to make do with what they have. Thereby, we can assure ourselves that we have not overlooked them entirely. In any case, we are forced to question neither the system nor the mobility mechanisms too closely. Certainly, this is not the rhetoric of hope and opportunity and sympathy which most poverty programs and proposals employ. The point is, however, that this is the consequence, intentional or not, that follows from the perspectives that shape such programs.

By contrast, when the problem of poverty is phrased in class terms, with a companion recognition of the inequalities it contains, then any solution demands a close examination of our society and its functioning. It is a disturbing examination because it may well require deliberate changes in social mechanisms and in those traditional beliefs that are not functioning as we had previously assumed. For example, I know of no definitive inquiry into the chances for upward mobility among the poor. Their aspirations for success as well as their patterns for socialization have been studied but not the realistic probabilities for their getting out of poverty. It is then little wonder, in the absence of such information, that we continue to rely upon older assumptions about the poor and about the nature of poverty. By not asking such questions we also seem to avoid any serious questioning about the nature of contemporary American society.

Significantly, however, some of the actions that have been taken by government do represent initial attempts at modifying existing patterns. In their own way, these attempts at change are nothing less than revolutionary. One can refer here to such programs, especially for blacks, as open college admissions, school integration, enforcement of equal hiring practices, and minority quota hiring in the construction trades. It is not without significance that these positive steps have been taken on behalf of blacks, whose militancy and organization have paid off at least to some extent. The unorganized white poor, by contrast, have won no such gains. Yet, the underlying significance of such programs is that they assume the existence of inequalities which can be overcome by some modification of existing social mechanisms. When, for example, college admissions are opened without regard to customary standards of high school performance, then we must accept the implicit assumption that public education is unequal for some segments of the population. When the federal government insists upon positive discrimination in order to raise the proportion of minority persons who are hired, then we must accept the assumption that previous practices were unequal, no matter what justification was offered to condone them.

Such actions have not been taken without social costs in addition to the economic costs. We have already seen the reactions of some of those classes most directly affected—reactions from the hard-hats in the construction unions, by the parents whose children must be bussed to comply with integration orders, and by the complaints from members of the middle class who must bear some of the economic costs and surrender some of their social privileges. Clearly, as even more serious changes are attempted to alter existing patterns on behalf of disadvantaged groups, then those in other classes will discover that the costs fall heavier upon them. Class privileges no longer may be so assured when they come under attack on behalf of the pursuit for equality. Potential class backlash undoubtedly is not overlooked by those responsible for developing new policies and programs for the poor. It is another cost that can well discourage any positive action. We must not lose sight of the fact, however, that Americans are facing a serious dilemma regarding equality—whether to change institutional practices so as to continue a search for equality in line with present conditions or whether to change traditional beliefs about equality to avoid paying any higher cost in class privileges. Either way, American society is not likely to stand still.

THE TYPES OF POOR

To a significant degree, poverty exists in the eye of the beholder. This is not to say that external facts are unimportant, any more than the art object is irrelevant to a comprehension of its beauty. Yet, the realities of poverty are perceived through a screen of existing attitudes that shape and give conceptual form to one's judgments. One man's scorn is another's concern, even though both rely upon external facts that are selected so as to lend support to their preconceptions. These remarks are by way of introduction to another aspect of poverty and inequality that should be considered—specifically, what the poor are like as seen through the filters of the three perspectives described above and what this means for programs of action. Although we have touched briefly on these matters before, they now should be considered in detail.

When poverty is defined only in terms of income, it is rather easy to separate the poor from everyone else, although this appearance of objectivity is misleading. Consider the following conclusion of the President's Commission on Income Maintenance Programs.

Any discussion of the poor must begin by defining those who are poor and those who are not. But it is obvious that any single standard or definition of poverty is arbitrary and clearly subject to disagreement. The standard which this Commission has employed is the widely used poverty index, developed by the Social Security Administration . . . based on the Department of Agriculture's measure of the cost of a temporary low-budget, nutritious diet for households of various sizes. The poverty index is simply this food budget multiplied by three to reflect the fact that food typically represents one-third of the expenses of a low-income family.[21]

The Commission, using this income base as just described developed the following poverty thresholds for the year 1968.

TABLE 3–2. **1968 POVERTY THRESHOLDS**

	POVERTY INDEX	
Family Size	**Nonfarm**	**Farm**
1	$1,748	$1,487
2	2,262	1,904
3	2,774	2,352
4	3,553	3,034
5	4,188	3,577
6	4,706	4,021
7 or more	5,789	4,916

Report of the President's Commission on Income Maintenance Programs, *Poverty Amid Plenty* (Washington, D.C.: U.S. Government Printing Office, 1969), p. 14, Table 1–2.

The point has been made earlier, and it has been repeated in the above quotation—that any income level is arbitrary and needs to be adjusted regularly to reflect changes in living standards and prices. This qualification is not a minor methodological problem but a serious conceptual one, for not only do prices change, but acceptable living standards are also subject to change. Poverty, entirely defined as an income problem, leads to an obvious solution of raising income levels enough to raise the poor—technically speaking—out of poverty; even so, everything depends upon the definition of poverty. In the conventional wisdom, this sounds like simple common sense, but such wisdom is neither accurate nor complete. As was previously indicated, the simple phrasing of an income solution has little likelihood of solving the problem because so little attention is given to the role of income beyond that of meeting subsistence needs. For example, not only is it important to increase income but also it is important to liberalize the manner of disbursing it so that the poor can increase their range of free choice. It is the difference between the stipulations attached to welfare payments and the freedom that is assumed from earning one's income.

The remedies that have been suggested do include a variety of programs, some of which are in the form of income assistance.[22] Others are aimed at job training, educational assistance, and "new careers for the poor" by creating new job classifications. The latter, perhaps, do aim at getting the poor into the labor force as relatively independent wage earners.

Those programs, however, are generally conservative in tone and intent because they look at solutions almost entirely within existing institutional mechanisms. Hence, income assistance programs do not move significantly toward an income redistribution any more than does the income tax. They are directed more at moving a proportion of national tax resources toward alleviating some of the most disturbing features of poverty, especially those exemplified by people living at or below minimum subsistence levels. I see them primarily as welfare programs that contain very few expectations for changing the poverty situation. The programs aimed at job and educational assistance also stay very much within accepted institutional patterns. Those who designed the programs seemed to be attempting, at most, to move some proportion of the poor into regular employment channels. In both types of programs I fail to find any kind of recognition that perhaps the existing economy cannot absorb these costs and demands. Thus, it will be necessary to move toward some serious reorganization of the economy, stemming from the knowledge that poverty is an integral, not an accidental, feature of our present mode of organization.

Yet, conservatism is not an inherent feature of the income approach, for it could be argued that a major income redistribution could be part of these programs. Such a redistribution would seriously alter the existing institutional structures and would serve as a kind of permanent Robin Hood solution. However few, if any, proponents of this view see it that way, probably because the majority of Americans are not poor and are not willing to sustain programs with massive social and economic price tags attached to them. Immediate remedies, in other words, must be ideologically compatible with existing values if they are to have any chance of being realized. Only in periods of massive crisis, such as wars or depressions, are we likely to allow any serious tampering with established economic norms.

Under such restrictions, I would maintain that the problem of poverty will remain because institutional causes of poverty are not taken into account. At best, perhaps, we might ameliorate some of the more disturbing consequences of poverty such as hunger, short-term illness, and housing. These are not remedies, however, and what is more they do not serve to reduce poverty in any lasting sense. The income approach, therefore, becomes dedicated more to dealing with symptoms than with causes.

If the income view of poverty seems superficial, then the cultural view appears as deep and intensive. For here we find, presumably, a deeper concern with the feelings and the cultural milieu of the poor.

The concept of a subculture is not new, although its application to the poor is a recent one. Kroeber, the famous American anthropologist, made detailed use of this concept in order to distinguish groups within the larger society, and he identified subcultures of races, classes, age, and sex groups.[23] The late Oscar Lewis coined the phrase "culture of poverty" in connection with his intensive case studies of Mexican families. An important element of Lewis' definition, sometimes overlooked, is that the "culture of poverty" is a universal concept meant to apply to many societies, or at least, to Western societies. However, many who now use this concept apparently do not include the broader international dimension that Lewis intended, insisting upon restricting it to the American poor. By this latter view, then, the poor are members of a distinct subculture, which like any culture, provides its members with a "design for living" and a "ready-made set of solutions to human problems," to use Lewis' words. The implications of this view of the poor have been fairly evident, and not surprisingly, have been unconsciously adopted by a number of Americans who perceive the poor somehow not only as deserving their position but also as beyond the scope of effective remedies. Conveniently enough, the poor are seen to behave in ways that are different from other persons, and at the same time, are seen to be socialized into those modes of behavior that are functional for them. As Miller and Riessman have put it, "If the culture of poverty is more than an interesting metaphor, it implies an intergenerational transmission of values and practices which inhibit constructive action."[24]

A particularly incisive essay by Arthur Pearl[25] identifies and then criticizes the implicit assumptions of the cultural view of poverty, and in so doing, illuminates how false those assumptions are. One argument Pearl identifies is that "the poor are victimized by an accumulated environmental deficit"—which is to say that they suffer from sensory deprivation. The research upon which this conclusion is based, however, is flawed by the fact that the rich and the poor respond differently to experimentation on this subject. "The popularity of the environmental deficit position," Pearl concludes, "is not hard to explain. . . . The onus is placed on the poor child, not on the inadequate institutions." Another argument is that "the poor are inadequately socialized." "The broken home life offers little social support. The child in that condition is unable to develop an adequate ego, thus he is not capable of self-sufficiency. The child, because of the absence of a father, cannot inculcate his social value system, thus he is prone to criminal activity and other social irresponsibilities." This thesis, like the first, simply lacks proof. It seems in this view that the conclusions always come to a conviction that "their condition is a consequence of their infirmity rather than a reflection of inequitable and inadequate social structure."

There are other criticisms to be made of the cultural view of poverty. First, I would agree with Valentine's critique that the cultural concept has been misapplied to the poor. "[T]he culture-of-poverty notion and related ideas contradict the all-important positive aspects of the culture concept. . . . That is, these formulations [popularizations of the culture concept] support the long-established rationalization of blaming poverty on the poor. Nothing could be further from the meaning, the spirit, or the ideological implications of the original concept of culture."[26]

Second, the use of the concept of a poverty culture overlooks certain realities that really are inherent in the concept of culture itself; namely, the possibilities for change. Hence, as Miller and Riessman have noted, "While many of these patterns and orientations are carried from generation to generation, contemporary influences are decisive in maintaining them. . . . Many of the poor are open to change, to taking advantage of new possibilities."[27] Yet, the way that the cultural view is advanced would strongly imply that the so-called successful adjustment that has been made by the poor offers little reason to change.

Finally, it can be argued that the perception of poverty as a subcultural phenomenon contains an inherent conservative definition of the poor and their role in society. It accepts inequality as an unavoidable feature of American society by allocating the poor to a separate corner out of which there is relatively little chance for advancement because the poor either do not want to escape or are incapable of escaping. To endow this culture, furthermore, with the positive function of allowing individuals to adjust to their condition indicates that these patterns of poverty become endowed with social legitimacy. The cultural view of poverty, thereby, not only recognizes inequalities but goes further to condone them and to rationalize them. By the same logic, one might just as well endow criminal behavior with the same legitimacy because the criminal, after all, makes a successful adjustment to a criminal subculture. I particularly like Lewis Coser's ethical comment on this point.

The notion of culture implies the notion of a desired and highly valued way of life. It is rooted in the idea that men belonging to a culture are devoted to it and give it their loyalty because it embodies for them prized qualities and valued virtues. But can a "culture of poverty" be valued and desired? Poverty is not a positive virtue. It is, instead, a negative condition that one wishes to escape. . . . To be sure, the deprived may present a variety of characteristics that distinguish them from the more fortunate, but they do not choose these characteristics or consider them admirable and desirable. They are in fact the mark of their oppression. It is ironic indeed to observe how life styles from which the lower classes suffer are transmuted in the eyes of liberal observers into admirable and admired characteristics.[28]

Given this interpretation of poverty, there is relatively little sense in trying to find remedies. Why try? What justification is there for attempting to change the culture of the poor if they have managed to adjust so beautifully to the reality of their situation? Moreover, one might even make the case that this evidence of cultural variety should be conserved, just as there is some justification for protecting the American bald eagle, the distinctive ways of the American Indian, and even the quaintness of the hill people in Appalachia. Therefore, it is possible to conclude that, from the cultural perspective, poverty need not be seen as a problem at all.

Both the income and the cultural definitions of poverty share a political conservatism that leads either to an acceptance of things as they are or to merely slight modifications of existing institutional mechanisms. The class definition of poverty, by contrast, leads to an inevitable recognition of the need for major changes in order to bring values and institutions into closer agreement. It has been pointed out previously that Americans will have to face the disparity between their beliefs and the realities of poverty and inequality.

By the class view, the poor are seen as being committed to their poverty because the forces that have shaped and changed American society have led to the present situation. Under present conditions, where mobility for that segment of the population has declined significantly, and where the inequalities of opportunity are evident, we find the poor locked into their position. It should be emphasized that this does not mean that the poor have adjusted successfully, but rather that they have no alternatives. What we may accept as the normal channels for upward mobility, such as education and occupation, simply do not exist for most of those at the bottom of the class structure.

It should be realized that the poverty rhetoric has been developed to help explain—without questioning the central value of equality—why the poor exist. Although we are confronted with considerable evidence of a class that is powerless, that has been created by our institutions, that is likely to remain and to increase in numbers, we seem to avoid incorporating these impressions into our language about poverty. David Matza, for instance, has described the matter in this way.

Disreputable poverty has gone under many names in the past two centuries. The major thrust and purpose of the word-substitution has been to reduce and remove the stigma, and perhaps the reason for its obsessiveness is that the effort is fruitless. In five years or so, if not already, the term "hard-to-reach" will be considered stigmatizing and relegated to the dead file of offensive labels. . . . Despite the difficulties in identifying and locating it, however, one may plausibly assert the existence of a small but persistent section of the poor who differ in a variety of ways from those who are deemed deserving. These disreputable poor cannot be easily reformed or rehabilitated through the simple provision of employment, training, or guidance. They are resistant and recalcitrant—from the perspective of the welfare establishment, they are "hard-to-reach."[29]

As with Marx's lumpenproletariat, the disreputable poor are beyond our efforts, perhaps even beyond our concern. They are thought to deserve their fate, probably because it is the case that by any reasonable standards they should be considered as the failures in a society dedicated to achievement. Perhaps the emphasis upon achievement makes the barely or moderately successful people afraid for the stability of their own position, so that they cannot look to the poor. Perhaps the belief in the inherent equality of the system releases us from any need to look. Whatever the reason, the tendency is strong to relegate the poor to a social position seen as a result of their own doing.

Yet, these simply are justifications that allow us to retain our belief in equality without close questioning. We must, however, begin to perceive the poor as a class of people that gives evidence of major problems within our own institutions. If there is a fault, then the fault involves not only those who suffer the consequences but also those who have produced them. Instead of dogmatically trying to avoid questioning our values and the possibilities of realizing them by placing the blame upon a class of people, we should consider those values and the possibilities for change.

This view may seem to be too radical, especially in contrast to the other two perspectives. Still, I believe that most studies of poverty have been too much concerned with the poor themselves and not enough with the forces leading to poverty; rather, we must move to redress some of imbalance currently evident in the analysis of poverty. The "problems" are less with the poor as such and much more with the forces shaping American society, even as these two aspects are inextricably interwoven.

A decided advantage for adopting the class perspective, for one thing, would be to reduce some of the current poverty rhetoric that assumes that equality values are still as vibrant as ever but that individuals are at fault for not taking advantage of them. As other writers have remarked, and as I have described above, our penchant for such terms as "hard-to-reach," "disadvantaged," and "culturally deprived" all are verbal screens behind which we try to hide from the stark causes of poverty.

For another thing, perhaps we might begin to analyze poverty and its solution along realistic class lines rather than along the value-laden lines that are so prevalent today. For example, Miller and Riessman have suggested that an outstanding characteristic of poverty is economic insecurity. Combining this feature with family instability, they go on to describe four different types of poor, thereby trying to get beyond the simple income definition.[30] The "stable poor" are those who have both economic security and family stability. At the other extreme, the "unstable poor" have neither. Between both are the "strained poor" who show family instability although they have a measure of economic security, and the "copers" who lack such security although they have relatively stable families. This typology is presented not because it can explain all there is to be known about poverty, but rather because it indicates a line of thought that should be encouraged. Unlike either of the other two perspectives, it is a feature of the class perspective that poverty is considered in its multidimensionality rather than in terms of only a single dimension. Family stability and economic security are two possible dimensions, and there is no reason why others cannot be identified and used to enrich the analysis.

We might begin to inquire, for instance, into the differences between the poor who still are struggling for upward mobility as compared with those who no longer are, or perhaps, never have struggled for that mobility. What effects upon their life styles and their concepts of the future are likely in view of such different orientations toward society? Rather than lumping all of the poor into a single, homogeneous category, therefore, we might begin to consider the dimensions along which the poor can be distinguished from one another.

From these remarks it should be evident that the class perspective of poverty introduces a vastly different set of possible remedies that can be included within the first two perspectives described. Essentially, this perspective holds that most other remedies, at best, are temporary because they do not aim at basic causes that have led to a poverty class. Further, I contend that we should be prepared to accept the possibility that more persons might be relegated to poverty in the future unless we seriously consider how basic forces are operating in American society today. Clearly, it is not enough simply to proclaim and to champion the pursuit of equality as we have always done without at the same time also making a sustained and deliberate attempt to discern how inequalities are produced.

THE FUTURE OF POVERTY

This chapter began with the question of whether or not the inequalities of poverty were likely to remain as permanent features of contemporary America. The concept of "inequalities" rather than the existence of poverty itself has been stressed. The central point, in other words, is not the matter of pauperism; instead it is the problem of social stratification and the permanency of poverty as a structural condition.[31] The poor, unfortunately, are always likely to be with us, but the critical point is whether poverty is a forced inheritance that creates a permanent class with a permanent membership.

The answer to the question of whether or not the inequalities of poverty will remain a permanent feature depends almost entirely upon one's perspective toward poverty. Hence, by the income view poverty is a temporary condition that can be remedied through programs to increase income, and thereby presumably, bring the poor into the mainstream of American affluence. By this view, it is assumed that the opportunity structure is still open and that income assistance or income maintenance programs can provide the required boost to overcome the economic inertia of the poor. The cultural view is not quite explicit with respect to details about opportunities and economic advancement. The definition of poverty as a subculture seems to carry with it the acceptance of current conditions, especially since it is accepted that succeeding generations born into poverty will become socialized into its culture. Yet, this perspective also carries the implication that a major revision of equality values should be developed. After all, if poverty gains legitimacy as a distinct culture, then its distinct values are also legitimate and the continued struggle for equality is not one of them. Finally, the stratification view contends that poverty has become a structural feature of contemporary American society, bolstered by the decline in mobility and the closing of the main channels for escape. Hence, current poverty programs do not get at the basic causes of poverty, but instead, they seek only to ameliorate some of its more devastating features.

All of the above perspectives, however, should be considered as views of poverty from the outside. Even Oscar Lewis' dramatic descriptions of poor Mexican families emphasized the impact of social conditions upon individuals. What we require, therefore, is some insight into the motivations and aspirations of the poor themselves as far as equality and opportunity are concerned.

The conventional wisdom, of course, holds that the poor probably deserve their poverty. Presumably they must be unmotivated, lazy, and without ambition, for otherwise they too would be able to rise out of poverty as countless other Americans before them have done. By this view, the structure is still sound; only the poor are at fault.

Unfortunately, the data available to answer questions relating to the inheritance of poverty are sparse. Yet, the available information definitely does show that, in general, the poor are indeed motivated toward success even though that motivation is understandably weaker than for those in other classes. In effect, both the conventional wisdom and the culture of poverty view are, at least, partially incorrect in defining the poor as being motivated by reasons that do not reflect the general values of equality and opportunity.

Beliefs About Opportunity

Rytina, Form, and Pease, in a study of adults in Muskegon, Michigan, sought to determine beliefs about opportunity, and they analyzed their findings by class and race as shown in the following table.[32]

TABLE 3-3. **BELIEFS ABOUT CHANCES TO GET AHEAD AND TO GO TO COLLEGE**
(in percent)

INCOME AND RACE	PLENTY OF OPPORTUNITY General	RICH AND POOR HAVE EQUAL OPPORTUNITY Income-linked	EQUAL OPPORTUNITY FOR COLLEGE General	POOR AS LIKELY TO BE IN COLLEGE Income-linked
Poor				
Black	56	11	22	11
White	90	47	57	38
Middle				
Black	58	21 ˙	41	28
White	80	49	75	37
Rich				
White	93	57	96	43

Adapted from Joan H. Rytina, William H. Form, and John Pease, "Income and Stratification Ideology: Beliefs About the American Opportunity Structure," *American Journal of Sociology*, 75 (January 1970): 708.

The apparent conclusion to be drawn from the above table is that optimism is related to class and race. The rich and white are the most convinced of all persons that opportunities exist for everyone and that the poor have as good a chance to take advantage of them. This attitude is not hard to understand; successful people believe that success depends upon individual motivations and abilities and that the opportunities are the same for everyone.

The more relevant and intriguing observation to be derived from the above information, however, is the relative optimism of the poor. Poor whites, for example, are almost as convinced as the rich that there is plenty of opportunity to get ahead, and the majority is convinced that there are equal opportunities for college. Further, 47 percent of this group also answered the following question in the affirmative: "Do you think that a boy whose father is poor and a boy whose father is rich have the same opportunity to make the same amount of money if they work equally hard?" The poor blacks are the most pessimistic of all, although the majority accepts the existence of opportunities. Finally, mention should be made that blacks, both poor and middle-class, are more pessimistic than their white counterparts. Hence, the black poor are neither as sanguine about college nor about the availability of opportunities as are the white poor.

This relatively optimistic view among classes and races, however, was much more restrained when individuals were asked questions about occupational inheritance and mobility. Almost all persons accepted the view that occupational inheritance rather than open mobility was the rule. At most, 10 percent of the white poor believed that the son of a blue-collar worker was likely to become an executive. From the other side, no more than 19 percent of the black poor believed that the son of an executive was likely to slip down into a blue-collar occupation.

My own studies of adults in New Orleans have yielded conclusions similar to those just described as far as the aspirations to get ahead and to succeed are concerned.[33] A sample of adults in the city was asked to indicate their relative willingness to forgo ten separate considerations in order to take advantage, hypothetically, of a better job. The items to be rated were, among others, "learning a new routine," "keeping quiet about one's political views," "leaving one's relatives," and "endangering your health." This same scale of items has been used in other studies and with satisfying results as a measure of adult levels of aspiration for upward occupational mobility. The responses were scored and summed for each person, then grouped into three categories as shown in the table below.

TABLE 3–4. **AVERAGE LEVEL OF ASPIRATION SCORES**
            (in percent)

Race and Class	AVERAGE ASPIRATION SCORES		
	Low	Medium	High
White poor	43.9	32.5	23.6
Negro poor	19.9	41.5	38.7
White working class	21.0	40.2	38.8
Negro working class	21.3	47.8	31.3
White comfortable	24.7	41.2	34.0
Negro comfortable	25.1	50.3	24.3

Leonard Reissman, "Readiness to Succeed," *Urban Affairs Quarterly,* 4 (March 1969): 385.

Aside from the white poor, it is clear from the above table that all other classes and race groups hold quite similar levels of aspiration for success. In fact, the striking feature of this table is the relatively high level of aspiration expressed by the black poor, who are at the bottom of any scale of opportunities. This latter group, however, expressed a great readiness to succeed and was very similar in its beliefs to those described in the Muskegon study. The relatively low aspirations of the white poor, it should be pointed out, can be traced to the fact that this group was generally much older than were any of the other groups interviewed. With the effects of age removed, I am convinced that the aspiration levels of even the white poor would be higher. In sum, the two studies just described point to a similar conclusion—that the poor are rather strongly motivated toward success.

Under these circumstances, the interpretation advanced by Rossi and Blum is quite correct inasmuch that the poor should be given more credit for holding any aspirations at all, let alone such high ones. They have concluded "that a lower-status child aspiring to a college education has higher aspirations than a middle-class child of college-educated parents." Arguing along these same lines, one might then conclude that "differences among socioeconomic levels would be lessened or perhaps reversed, the lower socioeconomic levels showing higher levels of aspiration than the upper."[34]

If levels of aspiration are so respectably high and if the poor are really motivated to achieve success in line with our dominant belief in equality, then what are the reasons for their obvious failure? Here is where the rich and the poor differ in their explanations, according to the information collected in the Muskegon study. The data presented in the following table tell their own story, showing what the different groups think about "personal attributes" as a cause of a person's wealth or poverty.

TABLE 3–5. **PERSONAL ATTRIBUTES AS A CAUSE OF INCOME**
(in percent)

INCOME AND RACE	PERSONAL ATTRIBUTES ACCOUNT FOR		POOR DON'T WORK AS HARD	POOR DON'T WANT TO GET AHEAD
	Wealth	**Poverty**		
Poor				
Black	17	17	3	0
White	34	30	13	19
Middle				
Black	29	19	4	6
White	35	41	30	29
Rich				
White	72	62	39	46

Adapted from Joan H. Rytina, William H. Form, and John Pease, "Income and Stratification Ideology," *American Journal of Sociology,* 75 (January 1970): 713.

The first two columns of the above table (Wealth and Poverty) include all those persons who gave personal qualities as the reason why individuals are either rich or poor. Understandably, the rich are the most likely of all to attribute their own success and another's failures to personal qualities. As a rich white man told Rytina and her colleagues, "Inheritance is the exception today. If you have to generalize, it's the self-discipline to accumulate capital and later to use that capital effectively and intelligently to make income and wealth."[35] From this perspective, then, the poor lack such personal attributes and are not motivated to get ahead, even though we have seen that this last generalization about them is not substantiated.

The white poor are somewhat masochistic, according to the data just presented. One-third of them accepted the view that poverty and wealth are determined by personal attributes rather than by factors outside of the individual's control. The white poor recover somewhat from this position, at least in their strong denial that they don't work hard or that they don't want to get ahead. The black poor much more strongly reject the belief that success is a result of personal qualities. As one told the interviewer, "The rich stole, beat, and took. The poor didn't start stealing in time, and what they stole, it didn't value nothing, and they were caught with that."[36]

Some corroboration of these trends has been supplied in a report of findings by Joe R. Feagin, who had a nationwide sample of adults interviewed in early 1969 on the subject just discussed.[37] By means of a series of questions, Feagin determined what reasons people believe to be the basis for the existence of poverty, and he grouped the reasons into those (1) in which the poor themselves are responsible (2) in which poverty is due to economic and social factors beyond the control of the poor, and (3) in which fate, beyond the individual's control, leads to poverty. Of interest here are two findings regarding the kind of people who emphasize one or another of these reasons. White persons generally ascribe poverty as the result of individual failings (56 percent), while blacks generally contend it is due to factors beyond the individual's control (54 percent). Apparently, different income groups still see the main reason for poverty as due to individual failings. Hence, a majority of each of the four income groups that were represented blamed the poor themselves for their poverty. Some differences among income groups appeared in the proportions blaming social and economic factors; 28 percent of the lowest income group (under $4,000) expressed this view, while 16 percent of the highest income group (over $10,000) did so also.[38]

The central point, however, is the strong conviction of the successful—that the opportunity structure is sound but that it is individuals who are at fault. I agree with the conclusion offered by Rytina and her colleagues, but they do not go far enough in the light of their data. "Our data," they conclude, "confirm the hypothesis that the support of an ideology is strongest among those who profit most from the system which the ideology explains and defends, the rich in this case."[39] Their data, as well as Feagin's and my own, indicate an exceptionally and unexpectedly high level of belief in the very same ideology even by the poor, who profit least from it. One must conclude, therefore, that the ideology is deeply ingrained throughout all segments of American society.

The Dilemma

From the available evidence, there does not seem to be a problem of motivating the poor; they are already motivated. Are we as a society, then, prepared to convert these motivations into reality by altering the present structure of opportunities and conditions where it is required? Miller and Roby have argued correctly that a recognition of poverty as a form of structural inequality requires much more than simple income improvements as an answer.

Conventional poverty discussions are thin because they are cast in terms of nineteenth-century concerns about pauperism and subsistence rather than in twentieth-century terms of redistribution. . . . When poverty is viewed in the stratificational perspective, we see that the goal of bringing all families up to a certain income level cloaks disagreements about the relative importance of differing, often conflicting objectives. For example, at the level of objectives of efforts to change the stratificational system, are we seeking a classless society with only minor differences among individuals; or is the goal a meritocracy in which individuals have in actuality equal access to high-level jobs that are highly rewarded; or do we seek to connect an "underclass," which does not improve its conditions as much as the rest of the society does, into the processes that will begin to make it less distinctive; or do we seek to reduce the gaps in some vital dimensions between the nonpoor and the poor?[40]

For American society herein lies the current dilemma that is posed by the existence of such large-scale poverty. Through the social-scientific knowledge that has been gained, we have been forced to realize that poverty is no longer a simple or temporary condition through which some individuals may pass. But pass they will. Actually, we know that individuals born into poverty will very likely remain there—not so much because they lack the motivations to get out but because the structure of society has failed to deliver adequately in terms of its values of equal opportunities. Couched in these terms, the alternatives are clear: Either we begin to revise our values concerning equality, or we begin to alter the structure of opportunities so as to enhance the search for equality. No amount of goodwill, sincerity, or minor tampering can evade these alternatives.

4
Race and Inequality

THE BLACK EXPERIENCE

Being black in America means quite probably the inheritance of inequality in virtually every aspect of life that makes a difference. Much the same also can be said for Mexican, Puerto Rican, and American Indian people living in the U.S., but since a discussion of these minority groups raises other aspects of inequality, the discussion will be limited to blacks alone.* These are some of the hard facts of race and what it means to be black in the U.S. today:[1]

■ The chances are 1 in 3 that you will be poor, compared with 1 in 10 for white persons.

■ There is almost twice the likelihood, as compared with whites, that you will be unemployed and an even greater likelihood that you will be underemployed.

■ The chances are 1 in 10 of being a professional or a manager, compared with 3 in 10 among whites.

■ The chances are 1 out of 5 that, if you are a black woman who is

*In addition to cultural differences, these minorities also differ as to their numbers, which would complicate a comparative analysis.

TABLE 4–1. **COMPARATIVE PROPORTIONS OF MINORITY GROUPS**

	Number (In millions)	**Percent of Total Population**
Negro	22.3	11.0
Mexican	5.1	2.5
Puerto Rican	1.5	.7
Indian	.5	.3

Bureau of the Census, "Spanish-American Population: November 1969," *Current Population Reports,* Series P–20, no. 195 (Washington, D.C.: U.S. Government Printing Office, February 20, 1970). Indian population figures from U.S. Census, 1960.

working, it will be as a domestic; if you are a man, it will be the same chance that you are working as an unskilled laborer.

■ If you are between the ages of 14 and 19, there is about 1 chance in 6 that you are a high school dropout, compared with about 1 chance in 13 if you were white.

■ If you are a black mother, yours could be one of the 23 out of every 1,000 infants that will die within the first month of life, compared with a rate of 14.7 per 1,000 for whites.

■ For every 1,000 unmarried black women, there are 86.6 illegitimate births, compared with a much lower 13.2 for every 1,000 unmarried white women. The rate for black women, by the way, has fallen in the last decade while it has increased sharply for white women.

■ For every 100,000 black women, 849 of them have been the victims of a violent crime, compared with 164 white women. For men, the respective rates are 523 and 394.

These are but some of the vital statistics of black existence; they represent a portrait of unequal probabilities for death, employment, poverty, and education. However, bad as these statistics look, they show improvement in relation to the past, and in some instances there are marked improvements over conditions a decade ago. The situation for blacks in America has improved, but this appraisal engenders optimism only if you look backwards to the ground that has been covered. On the other hand there is, perhaps, pessimism if one looks forward to the ground that has yet to be covered to decrease the remaining inequalities.

Whether or not the situation has improved, the inequalities suffered by blacks have been colossal, ranging in a long history from public violence and deadly assault to the more subtle forms of discrimination, disregard, and neglect that have been part of the experience of other minority groups in America as well.

An era of slavery has been followed by an equally extended era of inequality and denial. For most of the period since emancipation, inequality was legally supported, as in the "separate-but-equal" doctrine in schooling and in the requirements for voter registration. Discrimination without legal sanction was as prevalent as legalized discrimination in housing or jury selection. The curious part of this situation was the fact that the inequality not only was admitted but also was justified on historical, social, and even genetic grounds. Certainly, this created the moral conflicts of the "American dilemma," yet most Americans lived morally comfortable in spite of these racial attitudes by which blacks were thought to be getting what they deserved. Decades of studies, of discussions, of intellectual enlightenment, and the like, did very little to persuade the majority of Americans that their attitudes toward blacks were learned rather than factual, emotional rather than scientific. Even today, I doubt whether most of these attitudes have been altered significantly, even though their implementation in action and behavior has been somewhat curtailed. Many whites probably continue to believe what they have always believed about blacks, but in a number of areas of community life they no longer can act on it.

THE GENETIC VIEW

Sooner or later, these attitudes find a basis in the presumed genetic and inherited inferiority of blacks. The presumption, familiar enough by now, rests first of all upon an erroneous definition of race, and secondly, upon a pseudoscientific interpretation of selected evidence to fit that definition. Although the substance of the argument will continue to change, I doubt very much if it will ever be put to rest entirely. As descendants of Africans, the general argument runs, blacks are considered to be members of a biologically inferior race, which, as one explanation had it, never evolved as far as whites because of a less demanding environment. I. A. Newby has summarized this strange logic very well in the course of his excellent analysis of the way some social scientists have come to the defense of racial segregation. "The white man evolved in the challenging, invigorating climate of the far north, where he was forced to think for himself, to plan for tomorrow, to reason, to organize, to brave the elements to conquer nature. In his case, evolution produced constant improvement and, ultimately, superiority. The black, however, stagnated."[2] After all, the "evidence" was clear just by comparing the standards of living of Europeans with the primitivism of African tribes. Even the transplantation of the black could do little to alter his genetic inferiority, the proponents of this view argued, as they pointed to the evidence of intelligence tests, crime rates, illegitimacy, and the like. Within this closed and circular argument, there was a ready rationale both to explain the unequal social position of the black and to justify it on presumed biological grounds.

For decades, there has been substantial evidence to the contrary—evidence revealing that the practice of racial inequality was the most likely cause of the very consequences attributed to some genetically presumed inferiority. The unequal position forced upon blacks denied them any access to the channels for improvement, so what we saw were the damning consequences of social inequality rather than any so-called pure genetic causes. By rejecting consistently any serious change in this situation, the majority could maintain its preconceptions without testing them. For example, the uncounted statistical and methodological critiques that could explain the generally lower I.Q. scores among Negroes on nongenetic grounds were rejected repeatedly by those who preferred to believe that such scores were valid indicators of inherited intelligence. With this assumption, no improvements in education were necessary because, if the differences were due to genetic inferiority, then there was little reason to do anything about the environment. As long as little was done to change the situation, there were no improvements in black I.Q. scores, and so the prophecy was always self-fulfilling.

The genetic argument, concerned with the inheritance of various traits and abilities, is by no means settled and dead even in the scientific literature. Most recently, the educational psychologist Arthur B. Jensen has reported that racial differences in I.Q. tests are not to be explained solely in terms of environment and learning, but rather depend also upon inherited differences. The failure, after so many years, to reach a point of relative scientific certainty about these matters comes from the enormous confusion and ambiguity that surrounds the definition of race, the validity of I.Q. measures them- selves, the inability to separate unequivocally the environmental and learned influences from some more or less permanent genetic material, and finally, the inescapable fact that these sophisticated and complex "traits" can only be known indirectly through the use of probability tests on behavioral symptoms rather than through direct genetic inspection. Given these conditions, it is fair to say that the debates themselves and the reactions to them are of more inherent interest than the actual facts, if we could ever determine them completely. Hence, the appeal to a genetic argument in order to support one's attitude for continued racial discrimination is more revealing about those making that appeal than almost anything else they can say. In the absence of firm and unequivocal evidence about the heritability of any of these relevant traits, the only justifiable position would be to concern oneself entirely with the existing behavioral conditions and to leave the genetic proof to those who are prepared to conduct further research.

Yet, it is clear that most Americans hold certain attitudes concern- ing race, and from this basis, they proceed to search out whatever justifications they can find to support them. As late as 1965, for example, a Harris poll reported that 50 percent or more of all Americans agree that "Negroes tend to have less ambition," "smell different," "have looser morals," and "laugh a lot."[3] Our progress can be mea- sured by the fact that these proportions were once a good deal higher, but even so, there is still a long way to go. Consider furthermore, that those attitudes were expressed in 1965, eleven years after the historic Supreme Court decision on racial integration in schools. Indeed, one is forced to admit that such attitudes are strong, lasting, and relatively resistant to the pressures for change.

The point that needs to be made here, however, is that racial attitudes among white and black are not really conducive to change, but rather, tend to hinder and retard change at almost every step. In part, this is the result of ingrained attitudes that lead to a rejection of most that is new and different in the matter of race relations. In part, it is the result of a continuous and tense polarity by which all participants seem to be convinced that one group's gain is always another group's loss. What is lacking is the positive willingness by the majority of all persons to explore the required changes and the motivation to make the attempt. Blacks and whites continue to insist, respectively, that only their particular attitudes are correct and proper.

1954—A TRUE TURNING POINT

Yet, considering the history of school desegregation there is still some basis for optimism in spite of the general reluctance to change that has been evident ever since the unanimous Supreme Court decision in 1954. Without any question, that decision inaugurated an entirely new tone and character with respect to the problems of racial inequalities and the solutions to those problems. A significant feature of this new line was to institutionalize the use of social-scientific knowledge—a timely step that served to raise it out of the professional journals and out of the human-relations bulletins and to bring it into the decision-making process at the highest level. This action by the Court represented a singular breakthrough in legal reasoning by according social-scientific facts a status they had never had outside of the academy. If racial inequality is to be weakened, the process will require a combination of judicial decisions, legislative action by the federal government, and the application of social knowledge about the causes and consequences of such inequality. Perhaps deeply ingrained attitudes will never be changed, but, through the above combination of forces, their expression in action can be seriously restrained.

The Decision

It is worth considering the logic behind the Court's decision in the following quotation because it establishes the new tone mentioned above.

Does segregation of children in public schools solely on the basis of race, even though the physical facilities and other "tangible" factors may be equal, deprive the children of the minority group of equal educational opportunities? . . . We believe that it does. . . . Segregation of white and colored children in the public schools has a detrimental effect upon the colored children. The impact is greater when it has the sanction of law; for the policy of separating the races if usually interpreted as denoting the inferiority of the Negro group. A sense of inferiority affects the motivation of a child to learn. Segregation with the sanction of law, therefore, has a tendency to retard the educational and mental development of Negro children and to deprive them of the benefits they would receive in a racially integrated school system.[4]

The Social Realities

Even though we are fast approaching the end of the second decade since the Brown decision and the clear intent of the Court has not yet been fulfilled, the reasoning and interpretation by the Court have served to alter much of the previous history of our approach to racial inequality. Federal legislation on civil rights, economic opportunities, and housing discrimination all followed from the Court's recognition of social realities in its decision. As a result, the rhetoric, tone, and intent of race-related actions has been different in the U.S. since 1954. At the very least, America has explicitly rejected racial inequality as a public act, and enlightened thinking has even stripped away a good deal of the false mythology by which we once surrounded that subject. In so doing, Americans were brought face-to-face with their own attitudes—an accomplishment of no mean importance considering the earlier dreary history of race relations in the U.S. Americans can no longer return to that period when racial attitudes were kept from public inspection and accountability and were surrounded by a cloud of public hypocrisy. I submit that the racial confrontations of the last decade or so, as much as anything else, are due to the increasingly open acknowledgment of racial attitudes that had existed for so long. As a result, Americans came a significant part of the way toward recognizing their dilemma.

It is noteworthy that the major stimulus and route for change in black rights was through legal institutions, and that, necessarily, individual behavior had to be changed in order to conform to the altered codes. Attitudes, by contrast, have not been so directly affected, but, as has been suggested, they have become more public in nature. In essence, the courts have served as the institutional channels by which these significant changes were begun. As the political scientist Kenneth N. Vines has correctly pointed out, "Courts differ from other political institutions in that they cannot explicitly initiate policy processes; but we have argued that courts do initiate policy changes . . . [E]ven though courts do not initiate policies, they can achieve the effects of policy initiation through emphasis on certain cases while handling others routinely."[5] Yet, we cannot legislate proper attitudes, and here is precisely where the conflicts over racial inequality have become focused.

The dynamics of change initiated in 1954 have resulted in the current racial situation with its confrontations and tensions. Not only have teeth been given to the demands of black leaders and their organizations, but also spine has been given to many segments of the white communities, which have increasingly become characterized by their deepening levels of resistance to black demands. At its inception, no doubt, the desegregation of public education was more or less acceptable to white, middle-class liberals. By contrast, it was much less acceptable to white, working-class and lower-class persons who were in the forefront of the resistance to the Court's orders and to subsequent moves to enforce them. Although most of the initial violation of those orders has disappeared and although it has been revived in the recent resistance to busing orders, the situation of segregation has continued. The reason is quite simply the creation of various subterfuges such as segregated private schools or the enforcement of residentially segregated school districts in most American cities. In those drives, middle-class persons have joined members of the working classes and lower classes to prevent desegregation. Not to be overlooked, of course, has been the separatist demands by blacks themselves to maintain segregation for its positive political benefits.

With marked black gains, in spite of white opposition, there came the necessity to advance in other areas of social life in addition to education—the area in which the entire process began. Rising black voter registration brought the black more effectively into the political arena than ever before, a condition greatly aided by the very same facts of residential segregation that impeded school integration. Demands for fair employment and for quotas in hiring on federally financed projects were meant to bring greater economic prosperity and economic security to more blacks. College scholarships, followed by greater militancy and segregationist demands by black students also served to increase the tempo and scope of black demands. Success can be measured by the increased number of blacks enrolled in predominately white colleges: from 114,000 in 1964 to 378,000 in 1970. Success is also reflected in the rising proportion of blacks in such colleges as compared with a declining proportion in predominately black colleges.[6] In the sphere of legal justice, more adequate representation on jury panels was achieved, and, as a defense against charges of brutality, city police departments have been more careful in their treatment of black suspects. In short, the clamor by blacks for greater equality has achieved a scope that now includes most aspects of social life regardless of whether or not those demands have been met. It should be stressed that, no matter how far away from racial equality we still are, we have come a considerable distance in two decades, at least with respect to raising the level of attack upon such inequalities.

THE ROLE OF RISING EXPECTATIONS

Against the background of increased stridency in the rising expectations of blacks, more and more of the communities of the white majority have moved from sympathy, to disaffection and finally to downright opposition. Thereby, we have come almost full circle back to the attitudes that were held by the majority before 1954. The principal difference, however, is that blacks are much less willing to remain passive because the level of concern about inequality is considerably higher than was previously the case. Hence, white construction workers fight and shout at demands to institute black quotas in their unions. Similarly, white parents decry the lowering of educational standards and the disappearance of the community school as deliberate efforts are enforced to bring about racial balance. Landlords, suburban developers, and home owners resist the intrusion of black residents into their neighborhoods. The resistance is now expressed less by throwing bricks and more by inflating selling prices and by raising interest rates on mortgages. Even white college students, moving on their demands to change the governance of the universities and their functions, no longer have black cohorts because black students stick to distinctly black demands. The conclusion offered by the National Advisory Commission on Civil Disorders in 1968 after investigating urban race riots, may indeed have been prophetic: "Our Nation is moving toward two societies, one black, one white—separate and unequal."[7]

The prophecy is likely to be true because of the sheer fact of racial inequality in America, regardless of the reasons that have been given by the majority of whites. The conditions of life for most blacks, as the statistics presented at the opening of this chapter were meant to document, plainly are unequal compared with whites. Furthermore, these conditions are unique for blacks and should not be compared with the conditions faced earlier by immigrant minority groups. The reader should recall that some of the reasons listed below, as inventoried by the National Advisory Commission,[8] were applicable to the conditions of poor whites as well in the preceding chapter.

(1) *The maturing economy.* "Unlike the immigrant, the Negro migrant found little opportunity in the city. The economy, by then matured, had little use for the unskilled labor he had to offer."

(2) *The disability of race.* "The structure of discrimination has stringently narrowed opportunities for the Negro and restricted his prospects. European immigrants suffered from discrimination, but never so pervasively."

(3) *Entry into the political system.* "The immigrants usually settled in rapidly growing cities with powerful and expanding political machines, which traded economic advantages for political support. . . . By the time the Negro arrived, these political machines were no longer so powerful or so well equipped to provide jobs or other favors, and in many cases were unwilling to share their remaining influence with Negroes."

(4) *Cultural factors.* "Coming from societies with a low standard of living and at a time when job aspirations were low, the immigrants sensed little deprivation in being forced to take the less desirable and poorer paying jobs. . . . Although Negro men worked as hard as the immigrants, they were unable to support their families. The entrepreneurial opportunities had vanished. . . . Above all, segregation denied Negroes access to good jobs and the opportunity to leave the ghetto. For them, the future seemed to lead only to a dead end."

Regarding the last point, it has been pointed out in the preceding chapter and will be discussed later in this chapter, that blacks have internalized the desire for success in terms of the American message. Faced with considerably higher barriers than those faced by earlier immigrant groups, blacks continue to strive, probably with as much desire and willingness as did the immigrants.

The Commission concluded that, "Today, whites tend to exaggerate how well and quickly they escaped from poverty. The fact is that immigrants who came from rural backgrounds, as many Negroes do, are only now, after three generations, finally beginning to move into the middle class . . . Although some Negroes have escaped poverty, few have been able to escape the urban ghetto."

The more recent facts of the blacks' condition in American cities, coupled with the preceding history of inequality from Reconstruction and beyond, do not by themselves account for recent racial violence and tension. After all, such conditions have existed for some time, as have the violent outbursts of the past. The present situation is the result of a new confrontation, fed on the one side by higher levels of expectation among blacks, and on the other side by the hardening resistance of whites to any further acceleration of demands. From now on, racial struggles must be couched in terms of this dialectic, which is spiraling upward with growing intensity. Each increase in black demands serves to alienate another segment of white support, and in turn, stiffens the existing reaction. Each reaction serves to stimulate even more demands by blacks, so that the races are caught up in a dynamic escalation over which neither race has control.

One of the most concise and insight-laden statements of this perspective on the matter was offered by St. Clair Drake.[9] "How much violence of varied types can the social system tolerate," Drake asks, "without becoming dysfunctional?" He goes on to answer:

Violence has functioned as a "catalyst" and as a "danger signal" in the United States because there have never been any large groups within labor or among Negroes who espoused violent revolution for total reconstruction of the society. Because a relatively enlightened power elite is well aware of this, repressive violence has been used to "keep order" in specific situations, rather than to destroy the labor movement. The phenomenal growth of "liberalism," which commits the upper and upper-middle classes to the goals of a welfare state and to "fair play" for subordinated racial and ethnic groups, allows a wide measure of acceptance of pressure, including some violence, On the other hand, there is no guarantee against a shift in the direction of severe repression if militantly violent Negro groups expand and extend their activities, with the locus of the backlash being in the white working-class strata and finding political expression at the national level through the votes of the white lower-middle class—urban and rural.

Drake's previous sentence clearly pinpoints the dynamic stage of race relations (or racism) to which American society has now become heir. We have gone beyond the earlier period when racial inequalities were firmly accepted, or at most, were partially negated by sporadic and token actions by the majority in the spirit of a white noblesse oblige. No matter how pessimistic one may be about the results thus far, court decisions and federal legislation since 1954 have served to institutionalize national efforts to counteract inequality. These actions, in turn, have stimulated a level of organization and demands by blacks that are unique in our history but which have now become an integral part of it. The white backlash has become an inevitable part of this dialectic, fed by decades of racial prejudice and pseudoscience that sought to ennoble it. Yet, a critical fact often overlooked is that positive steps were taken, no matter how cynically one may view the pace or the reluctance with which they have been instituted.

THREE PERSPECTIVES TOWARD THE FUTURE

What then are the prospects for the future? Are we doomed for the next decade or more to spin through thesis, antithesis, and synthesis in a whirlpool of rapid changes? What will happen to the problems created by racial inequality and the problems created in the attempt to move away from it? Obviously, there is no easy answer and, certainly, not even any single answer. Rather, a good deal depends upon one's perspective which, in turn, defines the character of the problem and the direction for its solution. As argued with respect to poverty in the previous chapter, so here again with the subject of race, several alternatives are open.

Here it would be useful to consider three perspectives on racial inequality and the problems such inequality produces for American society. Although the substance of these perspectives necessarily differs from those described for poverty, they can be identified in a rather symmetrical fashion—income, culture, and class. As with the poverty analysis, the central concern here is with the varying definitions of the causes of racial inequality, and consequently, with the alternative solutions. Omitted from this analysis is the white segregationist's view, just as the extreme view of rugged individualism is omitted from the poverty analysis. Neither of these contains very much content that would enlighten the analysis except for some possible historical comparisons. Each view, in its own way, simply dismisses inequality as not even being a problem and thereby also discounts any need for change except to return to some romanticized past.

RACE AS INCOME

The first perspective categorized is income. Whether applied to race or poverty it contains a central assumption that, as far as equal opportunity and conditions are concerned, the institutional mechanisms are sound, requiring only some modifications to enhance their functioning. Applied to the problem of poverty, it should be recalled, this view led to minimal income-support programs that were meant to direct income to the poor so as to give them an initial boost. Applied to racial inequality, in which poverty is also involved, the objective is very much the same: to improve the income and income-producing abilities of the black population so that it can participate more effectively in the total economic environment. In both instances, the presumption is that equality can be achieved by raising the poor and the black to an effective entry level into the economic framework and thereby, into the institutional system. Indeed, to the extent that the problem of poverty is at the same time the problem of race, and vice versa, the objectives contained within the income perspective are the same; to solve one is also to solve much of the other.

The major sectors in which improvements are sought are those that were inventoried at the start of this chapter: employment, income, housing, health, and family conditions. On all of these counts and more, American blacks clearly are suffering from the effects of decades of inequality. More than whites, they are the unwilling recipients of more of the miseries and fewer of the benefits produced by a modern, urban, and industrial society. Quite clearly, it is racial inequality more than any other single factor that has led to this condition—a condition which has committed the black to the same position for generations.

Economic Power and the Income View

By the income view, the method of attack upon inequality is to direct programs for improvement specifically at blacks with the deliberate goal of bettering their economic position, either directly or indirectly. This orientation has led to such programs as job training which has been geared toward raising skill levels and thereby employment opportunities. The orientation has also directed funds toward educational assistance in order to keep blacks in school and to extend their schooling, and it has tended to stress "black capitalism." The last is a good example by which to illustrate the income perspective and is worth considering in some detail.

As the term suggests, black capitalism aims to encourage and to create, where necessary, the expansion of black business in the ghettos. The businessmen may be either individual entrepreneurs, partners or shareholders in ghetto cooperatives, or managers of national chains with a retail outlet in the ghetto. The intended objective, of course, is to keep as much income as possible within the ghetto and to keep it there for as long as possible. The argument has been made, with some economic justification, that white businessmen in the ghetto (and even black or white leaders of illegal operations) have funneled their profits out of the area with relatively little circulation within the ghetto. Hence, with greater black participation in the economic process, this condition could be corrected. For instance, the pressures upon whites to hire black people in ghetto-located businesses was meant to increase the money circulation, just as black ownership presumably would increase it also. The types of support for black capitalism are varied, including direct investment by whites, assistance in obtaining loans, and free consultation in management and fiscal practices.

Traditionally, black persons have had a monopoly on certain business activities for which whites have not competed, such as funeral homes, barber shops, burial associations, and life insurance companies. In some cities, this condition has created a rather small, black elite with interlocking economic interests so that burial associations, funeral homes, and insurance companies could be owned by the same small group. This economic base, furthermore, could and did become a basis for power both inside and outside the black community. In her study of a small city in the middle south (which is presented more as illustrative rather than representative), M. Elaine Burgess[10] identified 31 black, top power leaders who were presidents, vice-presidents, board chairmen, or other high officials in black businesses as follows: 6 in insurance companies, 4 in banks and loan companies, 1 in real estate, 4 in commerce and small business, 1 in a labor union, and the remaining 15 in the professions. The average number of local black organizations to which they belonged was 4, and the average number of memberships on boards of directors was 7.6. This group, like a comparable white group, was a minority that held power in the black community by virtue of its economic control.

Under black capitalism, the objective is to broaden the economic base and to increase the number of persons who are able to benefit from it. Under this rubric, several types of venture have been established—cooperative retail food stores, gas stations, and even some small factories to make toys or to assemble equipment parts on a subcontracting basis. A related trend has been to increase black employment in white businesses in the ghetto and to upgrade the positions open to them. All taken together, then, these efforts are meant to retain as much income as possible within the ghetto and to increase its circulation before it finally leaves.

Necessarily, this immediate goal also carries with it an intent to develop a greater commitment among blacks toward the established economic and political systems and to help forge as deep an acceptance as possible of existing institutional patterns and goals in the larger society. For one thing, it is presumed that blacks will develop a more positive view toward property and civil order if their own economic welfare is visibly and directly at stake. Yet, there was some question about the success of this belief during the long hot summers of a few years back when black-owned business establishments were also looted and destroyed along with those owned by whites.* For another thing, it is presumed that the levels of tension and resentment against whites will be reduced by the more visible participation by blacks in ghetto business activities. The success of these activities cannot as yet be determined. Yet, there have been properly high expectations of success among white business leaders who have been active in such programs and who see such programs as a force for possible changes. I particularly was taken with one of the lesser problems that was noted in a 1964 conference of business leaders on the subject. "One company in a large city in a border state, for example, must have two annual summer picnics because no park in the area can be used for a picnic for both colored and white employees. This is the way it is at the moment—but certainly we have to work toward the day when there can be one picnic for all employees."[11]

*Analysis of the information on the urban riots indicates that there may have been some selective economic retaliation by the rioters, although clearly, it is hard to establish that all rioters shared the same objectives. "According to most observers, the arsonists burned only stores, particularly stores which charged excessive prices and sold inferior merchandise. . . . The arsonists . . . bypassed shops which displayed signs reading 'Blood Brother' or just plain 'Blood' or otherwise identified the owners as blacks. This selectivity can be exaggerated: a few private homes and black-owned shops were deliberately destroyed. But, in view of the ferocity of the riots, what is remarkable are not the exceptions but the overall pattern and pervasive and intense sense of consumer exploitation underlying it." Robert M. Fogelson, "Violence and Grievances: Reflections on the 1960s Riots," *Journal of Social Issues,* 26 (Winter 1970): 151.

Perhaps a significant increase in ghetto economic activity for blacks will lead to more positive attitudes. However, black militants in some cities have been organizing to rid the ghetto of all white-owned businesses in order to create a totally black enclave, and it is hard to see how these efforts will fulfill the expectations by whites of lessening tensions. Further, it is also possible that the efforts of black capitalism will serve only to broaden the black middle class to some extent, without affecting the large majority of poor at all. If the latter is the case, I do not see why positive attitudes toward the economic system would develop as long as the economic situation for the majority remains as it is at the present.

School-Based Programs

The same manifest and latent objectives are also to be found in other programs aimed at blacks. School-based programs, for instance, have aimed at enhancing and extending the education of black children beginning with the preschool "Headstart" program and going on from there. The objective here is to inject educational improvements as early as possible in the child's experience and thereby to try to overcome his educational handicaps. Not unexpectedly, a recent evaluation of Headstart presents little cause for optimism. Although there were improvements among the preschool children in the program, these gains were rapidly dissipated by the early grades because other social influences did not continue and support the educational process as it does among middle-class children. Other types of programs such as "Upward Bound" or "Upgrade" have exposed students to museums, symphonies, and similar activities as a means to developing middle-class tastes.

Providing a Stake in the System

The point of these efforts is to bring blacks into the main society as much as possible and to develop a greater commitment among them to that society, after decades of relatively little concern or worry about such matters on the part of the vast bulk of the population. Necessarily, the efforts are discriminatory, aimed entirely at black participants, because it is argued that, without special support, the gap of inequality would never be closed. Generations of the kind of negative inequality of the past, thereby, are to be overcome by a strong effort toward positive inequality, or selective discrimination in favor of blacks. Understandably, such attempts, no matter how they are justified, trigger reactions among those groups who must relinquish something to make it work, whether it is white college applicants, white union members, or white home owners.

I do not think that racial integration is the foremost objective in such efforts, as much as it is a matter of trying to develop commitments to the American system by somehow converting the black into the mold of a white, lower middle-class type. Just as with programs for the poor, the gain is thought to be a society that functions with reduced tensions and frictions. If enough blacks can be converted now in this way, then succeeding generations will take care of themselves.

The foregoing is a naive view that omits an account of the dynamics that are, in fact, involved. First, it assumes that material improvements carry with them a set of attached attitudes of the type favored by the advocates. This is a false and dangerous presumption that is based on the axiom that "people who are fed do not make revolutions." We can but look at our aid program to Latin American countries to see that such is not the case, for people can be and are dissatisfied on ideological grounds as well—a condition which is likely to be a basis for revolution. It would seem to be self-evident at this stage in our history that the power a group holds, its convictions about its own destiny, and its belief in some standard of relative worth and importance turn out to be more relevant than material conditions alone. Of course, there should be a strong effort to improve material conditions, but there should not be the expectation that such efforts will be rewarded by the acceptance of the beliefs and ideals of the grantor. Yet, the intent of white leaders is to fit black leaders into their image; this is a serious mistake and constitutes the basis for the blacks' charge of racism. Second, any action to improve the conditions of blacks means some kind of sacrifice by whites—usually by those least able to make that sacrifice of money, privilege, or power. Hence, any significant step in that direction also primes a white response so that the course of change is, at best, a spiral of tension rather than a straight line progression.

On balance, I think the approach of modifying the tastes and values of the blacks is quite conservative in that it admits to only relatively minor adjustments so as to create as little disturbance as possible to existing institutions. Desirable and praiseworthy as this intent is, its realization does not seem to be a likely possibility in today's context of events. For one thing, the history of past efforts to improve life in the ghetto, at least since 1950, has been a history of almost stunning failure. Urban renewal, manpower training, aid to education, and model cities have not even approached the lofty objectives that formed and guided them. For another thing, as Sumner Rosen has pointed out, black leaders have questioned the intentions of the income efforts, and rightly so. He maintains that among spokesmen for black organizations there is "increasing belief that no real benefit to Negroes will come from programs that are financed, controlled and operated by the conventional agencies of government; these are seen as simply another aspect of a 'power structure' whose real interests are inimical with seeming improvement in the lives of Negroes."[12] As far as black capitalism is concerned, Rosen has correctly identified the conservative intention as one in which

development efforts, even if they do not make a meaningful impact, will nevertheless have the effect of validating basic capitalist ideas among ghetto groups. Since the failure of the economy in past decades to bring any meaningful improvement in Negro economic life has operated to weaken support for the American business system, such a prospect is an attractive one. It has the peculiar merit, from a conservative point of view, of buttressing the ideological foundations of the system while *reducing* the pressures for better performance by the business community in employment and service to the ghetto.[13]

The black leadership presumably can see that this is hardly a solution, for "what the power structure gives, the power structure can take away."

At best, then, the income approach toward racial inequality might improve some material conditions for some blacks. Even in this instance, however, a higher and more sustained level of commitment is required than the federal government and American citizens are willing to consider. We do not seem ready to tax ourselves to the extent necessary to show clear material gains for most blacks. Above all else, however, this approach is based on the narrow assumption that positive values and attitudes toward the economic system will be the automatic result of efforts to improve the ghetto residents' conditions. Such a change in attitude might occur, but, on the other hand, it might also help to develop a strong black community that opposes everything else around it. If we know anything at all about attitude change, it is that such change is neither simple nor obvious, but, instead, it follows a complex logic of its own.

Rosen has proposed that new forms of organization and delivery of health, education, employment, and the usual inventory of social services be tried in the ghetto as a kind of laboratory in order to benefit the entire society. "Innovations born and nurtured in the ghetto," he suggests, "will provide all of us with services superior to those we now have, in many cases at less cost. . . . In this context economic development in the ghetto is part of the larger strategy for transforming all of the major institutions of our society that affect the lives of people.. . ."[14] I would agree, but this objective seems to me to be far beyond the expectations of intentions of those who defend an income and income-related strategy.

Possible Flaws in the Income Approach

The income perspectives does not really provide scope beyond the immediate economic present. It is committed to developing support among blacks for existing institutional structures and mechanisms, thereby avoiding the sort of massive institutional changes that Rosen has suggested as an alternative.

Furthermore, it also leaves untouched the existing attitudes of the white majority toward racial inequality, and sooner or later these attitudes must come into play and become significant. For instance, just as the working class now feels threatened by the heavy dedication of resources to the poor, so too are many whites feeling threatened by a heavy dedication of resources to the blacks. The majority of whites, presumably, do not want racial violence, but neither do they desire tranquility to an extent that would seriously threaten their own resources and privileges. The resentment by whites, for example, to black quotas in the construction trades—quotas designed to overcome inequalities—have become evident in the newspapers. Without changing basic attitudes and beliefs, then, we inherit trouble from both sides of the racial fence. For the black leadership, at any rate, income attempts at change are meant to induce blacks to accept the present social system as it is or, at most, virtually unchanged. For growing numbers of whites, at the same time, the income attempts are a drain upon their resources and seem to make a mockery of their efforts to succeed, especially as black demands spiral upward with each concession.

I would fault the income approach with two basic errors. One fault rests with the assumption that income improvements for blacks will necessarily result in the creation of stronger commitments on their part to the American system. A second is the assumption that whites will accept this attack on their position and their resources without developing strong counter-attitudes.

Even so, I am convinced that we will continue to pursue and even to expand such income-related programs because no other alternative can be considered by those who are in a position to make these decisions. Such programs give the feeling that something is being done, when in fact, the core problems of racial inequality are not even approached. In this respect, the charges of racism made by blacks have a realistic basis precisely because such programs aim at co-opting blacks into the structure, but on the terms set by white leaders and for the purposes envisioned by those leaders.

RACE AS CULTURE: VIEWS FROM THE OUTSIDE

A cultural perspective of racial inequality that is similar in some respects to that described in the case of poverty can be identified. A significant difference appears, however, when the scheme is applied to race. The difference is that two interpretations with distinct consequences develop. The first, which I have called "views from the outside," has been developed largely by whites and is generally critical of the "black culture" as a satisfactory mechanism for adjustment. Unlike the culture of poverty which was seen as functioning positively for the poor, the black culture is assessed negatively as being dysfunctional. The second, "views from the inside," is a positive reading of black culture, mostly defended by black militants, and it takes the form of a black nationalism. The following section includes a discussion of the second interpretation.

A goal that I see as implicit in the cultural view held by whites is one of trying to inculcate white, middle-class values into black communities and to bring those communities more into line with the national culture. The attraction of a distinct subculture seems not to be as appealing here as it was in the view of the poor, so that major emphasis is placed upon the dysfunctions of black culture. To be sure, some positive elements of black culture are recognized as functional and worthy, as was true for the poverty culture. For instance, language and some of the experiences of ghetto blacks are praised as cultural items; such gestures are, in actuality, a modern version of slumming. For example, an I.Q. test based on these characteristics was publicized not long ago. It showed that white, middle-class persons scored about as poorly on this test as blacks from the ghetto did on standard I.Q. tests. The obvious message behind this exercise is to show that blacks have adjusted to their environment, as the ghetto I.Q. test shows, and it is unfair to expect them to score high on standard I.Q. tests that are based on a different set of experiences.*

Along the same lines, blacks are praised for their music, literature, dress, and soul food as distinctive and positive cultural elements. In fact, the readiness with which some whites have taken on some of these cultural items symbolizes their positive recognition of a black culture, and simultaneously, their orientation toward integrating parts of it into their own. The takeover of cultural items by whites shows the consequences of this dual goal. On one side, it contaminates the item (language, food, dress, etc.) much in the same way that an outcaste can defile the Brahman's food. Such items which become adopted by whites, necessarily must lose their value to blacks. On the other side, it further alienates the black culture devotee who wants to preserve cultural distinctiveness in a form separate from whites.

The Black Family

At a more mundane level, the greatest effort by those who hold the cultural view of race seems to be directed toward the reshaping and restyling of blacks in line with white values. The black family is a noteworthy example of an institution of society that has come under scrutiny in this respect. The focus upon the family is not really accidental, for it is admittedly a critical agent in socialization, the process by which culture is transmitted from generation to generation. Furthermore, it appears to be the one feature of black life that by white, middle-class standards is the most "pathological," the most visible,

*There is substantial truth in this argument, as was mentioned earlier in the discussion of intelligence and genetics. Sociologists have long held, and correctly, that the I.Q. test is a cultural instrument administered in a social context. Professor Jensen's argument, to the contrary, does not avoid or evade these constrictions. Indeed a recent analysis of his claim that racial and social class differences are related to intelligence in a genetic fashion has at best been disproven and at least been significantly questioned, especially as it depends upon research by J. Money on Turner's syndrome—a genetic anomaly which results in a female who lacks one of the usual two sex chromosomes. See, Liam Hudson, "Intelligence, Race, and the Selection of Data," Race, 12 (January 1971): 283–92.

and the most costly in the waste of social resources. Even so, there are some who see positive functions here, although it is not immediately clear how far they are willing to go with this view. The rationale for focusing on the family is stated in the Moynihan Report: "The family is the basic social unit of American life; it is the basic socializing unit. By and large, adult conduct in society is learned as a child."[15]

No social scientist would dispute these statements on the central functions of the family. Certainly, the family is the primary socializing mechanism, and it is here that the child learns about his society and his place in it. But, this recognition is not justification enough to single out the family—black or white—as the critical institution above all others with which to begin an understanding of the race problem. Indeed, the economic or political institutions could just as easily be identified for this purpose—and with equally sound justification. Could it not be argued that an economic restructuring of the black ghetto, as discussed in the previous section, is of higher priority than the social and psychological restructuring of black family life?

Let us consider in detail the basis for the cultural criticism of the black family and the consequences of the life style of the black family. Above all else, perhaps, the black family, by contrast with white families, is distinguished more often by being matriarchal; that is, the family is likely to have a woman rather than a man as the head. From an economic point of view, of course, the absence of a male is likely to mean less family income than would be the case if the male were employed. The absence of a male, from a psychological point of view, means that appropriate role models are not present. Such role models aid in the normal personality development of the child, and therefore, children suffer when the models are permanently absent. Somehow, this abnormal condition contributes to high rates of illegitimacy, casual sexual relations, and is further abetted by having a working mother who is often not present in the house—all of which increase the depth of family pathology among blacks.

Several reasons have been suggested to account for these family patterns. Some have traced the pattern to the period of slavery when the mother and her children were considered the family unit. More recently, the migration of black males to urban areas has been identified as a cause for weakening the family, as compared with normal (i.e., white) patterns. Within urban areas, black male unemployment has been consistently higher than among white males, and the resultant economic instability is seen as contributing further to a decline of family unity. One feature of the black labor market has been that it is the woman, rather than the man, who can find employment. Hence, black men, without economic independence or stability, have lost even more power within the family.

Matriarchy as a Prominent Feature

Unwittingly, perhaps, welfare programs have contributed to the matriarchal trend. In such programs as the Aid-to-Dependent-Children, for example, the presence of an adult male in the house can disqualify the mother from receiving financial assistance. The answer, obviously, is for an unemployed male to leave since there will be more income without him, no matter what this may mean in social or psychological terms.

The indices of family disorganization under such circumstances are expectedly high, and the disorganization, in turn, serves to extend the same trends into the future. For example, illegitimacy rates among blacks have been consistently higher than among whites. In 1940, the rate of illegitimate births per 1,000 unmarried women age 15–44 was 35.6 for blacks, compared with a rate of 3.6 for whites. In 1960, the comparable rates were 98.3 and 9.2. In 1970, the rate for blacks was 86.6 and for whites, 13.2. These are wide and significant differences even though the trends since 1960 show a slight decrease in the black rate and a slight increase in the white rate.[16]

The effects of this trend appear also in the distribution of family types since 1950 as shown in the table below.

TABLE 4–2. **COMPOSITION OF FAMILIES**
(in percent)

Year	HUSBAND-WIFE		OTHER MALE HEAD		FEMALE HEAD	
------	Negro and other races	White	Negro and other races	White	Negro and other races	White
1950	77.2	88.0	4.7	3.5	17.6	8.5
1955	75.3	87.9	4.0	3.0	20.7	9.0
1960	73.6	88.7	4.0	2.6	22.4	8.7
1967	72.6	88.7	3.9	2.1	23.6	9.1
1968	69.1	88.9	4.5	2.2	26.4	8.9
1969	68.7	88.8	3.9	2.3	27.3	8.9

U.S. Bureau of the Census, "The Social and Economic Status of Negroes in the United States, 1969," *Current Population Reports* (Washington, D.C.: U.S. Government Printing Office), Series P–23, No. 29, p. 70.

Evidently, from Table 4–2, a majority of *all* families, black and white, have both a husband and wife present as indicated by the percentages in the first category. However, looking at the last category, "female head," it can be readily seen that the proportion of black families is three times as high as for white families. What is more, the proportion for blacks has been increasing since 1950, with an overall increase over the full period of 10 percent. Further light on the situation is shed by considering the marital status of female heads of families by race as shown in Table 4–3.

The sharpest difference between black and white women is in the proportions who are separated or divorced. Among whites, 23 percent are divorced and 12 percent are separated. Among blacks, the proportions are reversed, with 13 percent divorced and 37 percent separated. These differences, most probably, are reflections of the cost of di-

TABLE 4–3. **MARITAL STATUS OF FEMALE HEADS OF FAMILIES, 1969**
(in percent)

MARITAL STATUS	NEGRO	WHITE
Total	100	100
Single (never married)	14	10
Separated or divorced	50	35
Separated	37	12
Divorced	13	23
Married, husband absent	6	8
In armed forces	2	3
Other reasons	4	5
Widowed	31	48

Bureau of the Census, "The Social and Economic Status of Negroes in the United States, 1969," *Current Population Reports,* Series P–23, No. 29 (Washington, D.C.: U.S. Government Printing Office, 1970), p. 71.

vorces, especially when separation can achieve the same objectives. In any case, half of all black families headed by a woman are the result of personal choice (separation or divorce) rather than the death of the husband. Among white families, by contrast, 48 percent are the result of the husband's death, and one-third are the result of personal choice.

In sum, the black family, more often than the white family, is likely to be characterized as having a female head separated from her husband and as having a higher rate of illegitimate births. The real question is whether that condition is pathological.

Black Matriarchy—Pathological or Just Different?

The Moynihan Report took the unequivocal position that it relied on the standards of the white majority as the basis for evaluation.

In essence, the Negro community has been forced into a matriarchal structure which, *because it is so out of line with the rest of the American society,* seriously retards the progress of the group as a whole and imposes a crushing burden on the Negro male and in consequence on a great many Negro women as well. [Emphasis added.][17]

But, it seems fair to ask, "Is it valid to use the standard of white society in order to judge black behavior as being pathological?" The answer is that very much depends on who is making the judgment and for what purposes. If the intent is to build a case for the majority norm because it is the majority, then any deviation as important as family structure must come out as being pathological. Yet, one's interpretation of the situation can have a lot to do with the conclusions reached. For example, one doubts that it was considered pathological for husbands to migrate to the United States from overseas at the turn of this century and to leave their families behind. On the contrary, it was taken as a sign of ambition. Are black men to be judged more harshly for similarly responding to economic pressures? The Moynihan Report stated a very definite view of this matter in the case of blacks.

There is, presumably, no special reason why a society in which males are dominant in family relationships is to be preferred to a matriarchal arrangement. However, it is clearly a disadvantage for a minority group to be operating on one principle, while the great majority of the population, and the one with the most advantages to begin with, is operating on another. . . . Ours is a society which presumes male leadership in private and public affairs. The arrangements of society facilitate such leadership and reward it. A subculture, such as that of the Negro American, in which this is not the pattern, is placed at a distinct disadvantage.[18]

The last quotation, it should be carefully noted, has moved the issue from the matter of "matriarchy" to that of "family relationships" and "male leadership." Even so-called complete families could well have a domineering mother, just as families without a husband could still have access to male role models through other kinship relations. In short, the Moynihan Report makes an unproven transition from the demographic reality to the psychological environment.

The publication of the Moynihan Report, which did not suffer the usual silence reserved for government documents, produced a flurry of controversy among black leaders, social scientists, and government officials. A book about the controversy, containing the original report as well, was even published two years after the Report.[19] Two distinct issues emerged from this book of reactions: (1) the evidence of family pathology and (2) the consequences of action programs.

The consequences for action, of course, follow rather directly from the particular stance that is taken regarding the black family and its strengths and weaknesses. As Elizabeth Herzog noted in her essay in the above-mentioned volume,

Both sides of the controversy agree that there is urgent need for strong action to increase the proportion of sound, harmonious two-parent homes among low-income Negroes. They disagree on whether that action should be focused primarily on intrafamily or extrafamily problems. The acute-crisis view suggests that primary attention be given to the family as such. The other view suggests that the best way to strengthen low-income families as families is to give primary attention to building up the economic and social status of Negro men.[20]

However, the more relevant issue for our analysis concerns the estimate of family pathology. Here is where the cultural view of race appears most clearly, and it should be given detailed consideration.

The opening quotation from the Moynihan Report fixed on the pathological character of the black matriarchy—a pathology that is presumed to develop because the black subculture differs so much from the majority white culture. The presumption of a pathology with regard to black matriarchy leads to the suggestion by Lewis Coser that whites can be blamed for imposing the matriarchal form upon blacks.

It is one thing to defend the right to diversity in life styles where such nonconforming and divergent patterns have been freely chosen, but it is quite another matter to defend a situation where such divergencies have in fact been imposed by those who occupy a superordinate position in the social structure. I know of no evidence to indicate that women who are the heads of matrifocal families desire such positions of their own free choice. They have been forced into these positions by desertion, by divorce, or by the insistent pressures of male unemployment and the inhuman stipulations of our welfare policies.[21]

Whereas the Moynihan Report seemed to be blaming the black family for its pathological form, Coser has placed the blame on white society. This view can now be extended further, as Frank Riessman does, not only by laying the blame on the larger society, but also by finding room to praise blacks for their adjustment to the situation (shades of the culture of poverty view!).

The basic defect in the Moynihan Report thesis is a *one-sided presentation of the consequences of segregation and discrimination.* That damage has been done to the Negro as a result of discrimination cannot and should not be denied. But the Negro has responded to his oppressive conditions by many powerful coping endeavors. He has developed many ways of fighting the system, protecting himself, providing self-help and even joy. One of the most significant forms of his adaptation has been the extended, female-based family. To overlook this adaptation and instead to emphasize one-sidedly the limiting aspects and presumed pathology of this family is to do the Negro a deep injustice.[22]

I am not certain about the "joy" or the "powerful coping endeavors" that Riessman credits to the black family. Nor is it thoroughly clear whether the effects of this argument would tend to counteract or to exacerbate the pathological features, but the point of the controversy is whom to blame for the black matriarchy, which, in turn, is the presumed case of the black pathology.

To complicate matters somewhat, one could introduce some information that brings the whole assumption of a social pathology in black families into question. As was noted earlier, most of these discussions have been based on the assumption that a matriarchal family must lead to a pathological environment. Herbert Hyman and John S. Reed[23] have brought this matter into doubt. They did a secondary analysis of sample survey data that contained questions about patterns of female and male influence—a psychological dimension that is much closer to a determination of family pathology than the demographic facts of matriarchy alone. The results were analyzed and tabulated according to the race of the respondent, and the information is presented in Table 4–4.

The Insights Gained from Research

The point that emerges clearly from the information obtained by Hyman and Reed is that blacks and whites responded very much alike to these questions. Where female dominance is high for one race, according to the Gallup survey, it is equally high for the other. Certainly, such data are selective, and perhaps they are even too general to be applied to so complex a psychological matter. Still, it is a step closer to the dynamics of the pathology than is a generalized imputation made about black families—an insinuation made solely on the basis of selected demographic factors such as the presence of a female head of the family or such as the rate of illegitimacy. Hyman and Reed's conclusions are conservative and realistic in the light of their evidence. "Our evidence is tentative, but it certainly casts the issue into doubt. If the concept of a culturally linked Negro-white difference in family organization has been weighty enough to generate debate about social policy and action, it deserves the conclusive evidence that primary research could provide."[24] Stated another way, these data should raise some doubts about the pathology of matriarchy among black families, particularly in view of other contributing factors in the environment.

TABLE 4–4. **PATTERNS OF MALE AND FEMALE INFLUENCE IN NEGRO AND WHITE FAMILIES**
(in percent)

Surveys and Questions	Negro	White
Gallup—1951		
Percent reporting that most important influence on them when growing up was:		
Father	27	31
Mother	73	69
NORC—1960		
Percent reporting that the important family decisions were made by:		
Father	28	23
Mother	14	13
Percent of married respondents with children reporting that decisions about child discipline were made by:		
Husband	4	7
Wife	37	28
Jennings—1965		
Percent of youth from politically divided homes who agree with:		
Father	32	34
Mother	40	40

Herbert H. Hyman and John S. Reed, " 'Black Matriarchy' Reconsidered," *Public Opinion Quarterly,* 33 (Fall 1969): 351.

It is impossible to resolve the differences on the evidence that is now available. There are assumptions and resultant questionable conclusions that should raise doubts on both sides of the issue. For one thing, it must be remembered that we are talking about some 30 percent of black families and not about *the* black family, as if there were a single uniform type. For another thing, along the same line, there are class differences within the black population so that the "pathology of matriarchy" may well be a lower-class rather than a middle-class phenomenon. Indeed, I very much suspect that such is the case. Further, what is the cause-and-effect relationship that exists between family structure and socioeconomic conditions? More than likely, both poverty and family structure result from the deeper cause of racial inequality, and, thus, I see no reason to applaud the blacks' adjustment to miserable conditions. Finally, even the implied emphasis upon male dominance as a positive good may be presumptuous because traditional human dominance patterns seem to be in the process of change; if that is the case, what happens to the view of matriarchy as pathological?

The point to be made in raising these questions is that the cultural perspective that focuses on family structure in black communities is a narrow one. Whether one evaluates family structure as pathological or as a positive functional adjustment, it is really an issue of less importance than the causes and consequences of racial inequality. Puerto Rican and Mexican families, presumably, do not suffer from a matriarchal family structure, but they are not much better off as a result. It must certainly be the case that, if blacks did not suffer from inequalities and were economically secure, then the type of family they have would not bother anyone; at the most, the nature of the concern would be of an entirely different order than it is now. By the same reasoning, I must assume that the efforts to change the black matriarchy, and thus to cure the pathology, are not likely to make much difference in the conditions of blacks if the causes and consequences of their inequality are left untouched. Rather, I am convinced that if the causes and consequences of inequality are removed, then the structure of the Negro family will become much less important as an issue for reformers.

RACE AS CULTURE: VIEWS FROM THE INSIDE

A quite different cultural interpretation of race is to be found in the ideology of black militants. The white, middle-class perspective just described emphasizes the black subculture and its pathology. Black militants, by contrast, see black culture as a positive entity that needs to be kept distinct and to be encouraged. Black culture, from this perspective serves as a primary focus for identification. It has political potential, which is its attraction—political potential that can be used to develop a separate and autonomous loyalty, much as nationalism has been used as a guiding ideology by revolutionary independence movements in the new nations.

There are different motivations and varied objectives that can be included in this category, ranging from the paramilitary Black Panthers to much less violent black organizations. However, the common thread that unites them in theory, although not always in action, is one of black separatism. The objective is not, as we saw before, to seek ways by which blacks can adjust successfully to white society, but instead, to create and sustain a separate black power base. There are differences, however, in the long-range objectives of this separatism. One view holds that a developed sense of black identity must be established before the black should even try to become integrated into the national society. It is a bargaining theory that successful negotiations can only be developed from strength, not weakness. Therefore, to begin seeking integration at once, as white liberals have been urging for so long, would leave blacks dependent upon whites and deprive them of the needed political strength by which independent gains are to be achieved.

By contrast, another group that also assumes the necessity of a separate black culture and of separatism does not seek integration. Instead, this group would seek to maintain racial segregation through the form of an independent, autonomous, and equal black group somewhat like that of other racial and ethnic groups in America. Harold Cruse, one of the most publicized spokesmen for this view, has drawn an explicit analogy between the ethnic identity of such groups and the separatism of the black that he supports.[25] The black, he contends, has relatively few rights because his ethnic group holds relatively little power. "Very understandably these people want to be full-fledged Americans, without regard to race, creed, or color. They do not stop to realize that this social animal is a figment of the American imagination and has never really existed except in rare instances."[26] In reality, Cruse contends, every American is a member of some group such as "white, Anglo-Saxon Protestant," or "white Catholic," or "white Jew." These groups do not seek to become integrated, but instead, seek equality through the power that they can exert as members of such groups. Clearly, then, for the black to abandon his identity now in pursuit of the integrated society would mean that he would surrender his strength and probably any chance of achieving an equal status with whites.

There is a wide chasm that separates black militants from white liberals, even though both contend that their objective is to achieve equality. For the latter, the means leading to cultural integration are less important than the goal itself. For black separatists, on the contrary, it is the means that are of primary importance because the success of the goal depends on them. Therefore, the development of a viable base for political power and control must get the highest priority.

Cultural distinctiveness, as seen by the separatists, becomes a mechanism and a technique for building group consciousness with political effect. Any cultural item can help to serve the purpose if it is uniquely identified and is widely accepted by the group, such as dress, hair style, language patterns, food, and so on. Furthermore, a cultural heritage that has originated in Africa encourages one to build on the separation from American culture and from its inevitable connection with slavery. To relate black history as originating in slavery is to set blacks into a subordinate status from the very start, which is no way to begin the development of cultural pride. The purpose of creating and expanding this kind of cultural identity, then, is to develop a power base that is viable. If necessary, white society can be used as the foil to help create a type of "negative nationalism" which, in turn, gives blacks a sense of greater identity with each other by contrast with the whites outside.

Political power, however, is never the prerogative of one group acting alone; one must take into account other groups that are competing for the same things. Black separatism may be successful in mobilizing a unified political bloc, especially in the urban ghettos where they possess majorities. Within limits, such power can be used in an institutionalized manner, as for example, in the election of black mayors, councilmen, and school board members. It could also be used as a base for mobilizing power even more broadly through pressure on decision makers at state and federal levels. In either case, the white reaction sooner or later appears, moving to quarantine black power if it is believed to be too threatening. This could be accomplished by moving the centers of decision making to ever higher levels—levels that are beyond the reach of local black communities. The trends are already obvious.

In any case, all of these power plays involve action and reaction, and they are national rather than being strictly regional or local in scope. We are a national society. The majority of significant decisions have moved from local to national levels, and it is here that the seat of power is to be found. An interesting twist is that, although the election of black, big-city mayors is a local event, it is one that transcends local limits. Not only does that fact have significance for black political power on the national scene, but, in addition, the role of the federal government in the cities elevates some local elections into broad national importance. It would be useful to review some of the past conditions that eventually produced the trends that have sparked that national importance.

From Reconstruction until 1954, American society could be characterized as having what Leo Kuper identified in South Africa as a "parallel racial structure" by which blacks and whites were separate, unequal, and with blacks under political domination by whites.[27] Since 1954, American society has moved from that type of structure and toward an "intercalary racial structure" in Kuper's terms, which means that, although still separate, the racial groups move to coordinate their activities, such as using black policemen for service in black ghettos, especially during periods of tension and violence.[28] The change is not over yet, so the coordination is very haphazard, confused, and often misunderstood because racial contacts and relationships have not been institutionalized. Whites continue to seek control on their own terms, only relinquishing elements of this control temporarily and only when they are placed under pressure.

Black Leadership and Frustration Politics

Blacks, on the other hand are experiencing their own crises of leadership so that the kind of racial coordination mentioned has not yet been developed even in view of the relative success of the National Black Convention. On one side, as Bayard Rustin has remarked:

The younger Negroes are engaged in "frustration politics" and in "frustration economic thinking." Stokely Carmichael is not a reverse racist. What he is saying is that "all of these years we've wanted to be friends with whites; all you've done is to hurt and insult us. OK I don't want to be friends with you; get out of our way; you are Whitey; you are Hunkey."[29]

In the same interview, Rustin goes on to point out, "The danger is that the Negro is contracting out of the political process. The militant young Negro is unconsciously engaged in helping develop 'a coalition of opposites': strengthening the reactionary forces."

On the other side, the black establishment leaders are caught in the middle. As Colin Legum noted after his interviews with black leaders,

The dilemma of the black [e]stablishment is posed by the conflicting demands on it by the ghetto-dwellers and the white political system calling for two different roles. . . . The ghetto-dwellers want the middle class to identify themselves uncompromisingly with their ghetto-centered aspirations in order to provide a unified black challenge; while the white [e]stablishment looks to them to act as a delaying political mechanism to achieve painless, gradual change. Thus the black bourgeoisie are essentially the "men in the middle."[30]

The young black militants, those who challenge both the black and the white establishments, are trying to create a hard cultural identity as an expedient political device. As with the "negative nationalism" of colonial peoples reaching for independence, such a route may have the immediate advantages of building instant cohesion; the costs for the future, however, are high. For one thing, a threatened white power structure can react instinctively out of fear, bringing down greater repression and inequality than were present before. For another thing, sooner or later negative nationalism must become positive if it is to succeed. This means that significant numbers of blacks must succeed within the value standards of the majority culture, not within those of the minority. Black pride, black history, and black culture can help develop a sense of identity and a sense of purpose, but they do not provide enough background to use mathematics, to practice medicine, or to become a successful business entrepreneur, or for that matter, to perform any other job that spells success and independence. Nor is it realistic to respond that such success is useless, pathological, and not deserving of anyone's ideological attention. If the objective of black leaders is to attain a viable identity from which to help shape changes toward equality, they are better off having attained a solid base in the existing system than staying forever outside of it.

A Review of Perspectives from the Inside

It is possible to summarize briefly the alternative positions that have been described. On the other hand, it is impossible to predict at this point in time which one is likely to become reality in the next decade because there are many complex variables involved in that determination.

1. *Separatism to Separatism.* This is the view that seeks to nourish black cultural separatism and identification and to sustain them in the future. Here is where the ideology of most black militants would be included.

2. *Separatism to Integration.* This is the view that foresees an end to separatism and the beginning of the development of greater racial equality through coordination between black and white groups, a coordination that can be characterized as mutual respect. The present objectives of building black identity are the means to redress some of the existing racial imbalances and to provide greater bargaining strength for future gains. Unlike the black cultural view, this view foresees significant class gains for blacks so that they will become integrated into the national society.

3. *Integration to Integration.* This is the view that blacks should work within the white society as much as possible in order to achieve equality in the future. Basically, it is a conservative argument that eschews any effort to build black separatism and to capitalize upon it. Those who hold this view fear that, once separatism is achieved, it will never be dissolved and, therefore, should be avoided. It is a view shared by older black organizations and by many white liberals—the principle that equality can be achieved through existing institutional mechanisms without creating tensions and violence.

In the case of the three positions described above, each implies its own type of social problem for the future. The move toward separatism, whether short-range or long-range, obviously implies some need for major alterations in existing institutions. The stress upon working within the system, by contrast, simply overlooks the growing frustrations and impatience among blacks, especially the young blacks, who have developed rising expectations during these years of change. Furthermore, throughout all of this, there are the real struggles for leadership in black communities as evidenced by the emergence of political splinter groups. At the same time, each struggle and demand by blacks creates its own white backlash, which is likely to become stronger with each growing demand. There is no single, straight-line trend. Lewis Killian, in one of the most thoughtful analyses of black militancy and its future has identified several competing trends.

The new radicals among Negro leaders are playing a . . . dangerous game. . . . There is every indication that the white electorate and its elected representatives will react to continued threats and to more violence in the streets not by a renewed effort to understand and alleviate the plight of underprivileged Negroes, but by reactionary measures to suppress these disorders. . . .

Assessment of the countervailing power that the white [e]stablishment could muster to oppose even the best organized revolution of Black Power makes the Negro Revolution seem indeed to be the Impossible Revolution.[31]

I must agree with Killian's pessimistic conclusions. The militants' objective of trying to build a form of cultural nationalism based upon a black subculture is fraught both with potential and with real conflict on all sides. Within the black communities themselves there is the immediate prospect of struggle for leadership, and, from the white communities, there is the immediate prospect of backlash. This problem has been simply defined by G. Franklin Edwards: "The conventional leaders of the past won't be accepted by the militants, and the militants are too rigid to deal with the white community."[32]

RACE AS CLASS

The weaknesses inherent in the cultural perspective, whether of the white-liberal or black-militant variety, become more apparent when seen against the third perspective of race as class. Briefly, this view identifies class as a primary factor for understanding the nature of racial inequality; it posits the need to enlarge the race concept, so to speak, in order to couple the concept with a class designation in much the same way as in the analysis of white groups. Race is an important social category, of course, but it is no more all-encompassing in the case of blacks than it is in the case of whites. Rather, the only justification one might give for generalizing to all blacks is that so high a proportion of them are poor and in the lower class, whereas in speaking of whites we usually add differentiating class criteria such as "lower-class," "middle-class," and the like. The sloppiness of the generalization about blacks, however, should not be accepted as valid, and this becomes especially clear when attention is turned to the dynamics and trends within black communities themselves and to the future of racial inequality.

Class Rather Than Caste

One of the earlier class analyses of race was that by Oliver Cox. The work appeared in 1948, somewhat before the current developments.[33] Cox disputed a formerly popular idea among social scientists—that the blacks should be considered as a separate *caste* that is distinct, identifiable, and similar in form and function to a typical caste in the Hindu system. The caste interpretation, as described by W. Lloyd Warner and his students, was based on studies they had conducted in the South, where they found blacks living in what was a dual society sharply divided along a race line. The barrier between whites and blacks in the South attained its castelike form by being institutionalized in a number of ways that regulated behavior, especially in legal prohibitions against intermarriage and interracial education and in social prohibitions against most forms of interracial contact involved in eating, in transportation, and in public gatherings. Contacts across racial lines were quite specifically controlled by law and by custom. In spite of such manifestations, however, Cox rejected the caste explanation and contended that the basic values supporting Hindu caste divisions and contacts did not apply to American society. One of his strongest arguments, for instance, was that the American stress on equality, even if only formal, gave no support to a biracial caste system, even though castelike barriers existed and were institutionalized in some sections of the country. The Hindu caste system, by contrast, relies heavily upon institutional supports stemming from a religious rationale that emphasizes the idea of ritual pollution. In India, most social contacts across caste lines are severely proscribed by a series of complex rules meant to keep the higher castes safe from the possibility of social contamination by members of the lower castes through establishing physical avoidance in every instance. In the U.S., such rigorous isolation for the avoidance of ritual pollution did not exist because there were some forms of physical contact. For instance, blacks handled both the food and the children of whites—an intimacy that would be inconceivable in a true caste situation. Intermarriage was illegal, of course, because of fear of pollution, except that white males could and did father offspring with black women. Often the fathers did not take any responsibility for the illegitimate children. The two situations—India and the old American South—are analogous, but there were critical exceptions.

For this and similar reasons, Cox argued that American race relations had to be seen in relation to a class, rather than in relation to a caste system. In effect, he explained, blacks were kept in the lower class so as to provide a cheap and available labor supply that could be kept under tight control. For economic purposes, then, blacks were little more than an indentured class serving the needs of a white economy. Castelike features were present, both as part of the slave tradition and as part of the postslavery economy, but they were not the clue for understanding the black position. The important feature of the argument for Cox's view was that it pointed to the need for blacks to improve their *class* position rather than being so totally concerned with altering the ritualistic caste aspects. Once their class situation was improved, then the manifest caste aspects would soon become unimportant.

Taking this cue, then, a class view can be developed in which the predominance of blacks in the lower class in America becomes a pivotal characteristic. Hence, to understand not only the events and developments within black communities, but also to consider solutions to racial problems requires a full appreciation of the class lines that divide those communities. For instance, as shall be described later, the gains recently achieved by blacks can easily become translated into advances in upward mobility—a process by which an increasingly large proportion of blacks move out of the lower class and into either the working class, the lower-middle class, or the middle class. The opening of college admissions and the pressures to enforce discriminatory hiring in favor of blacks for college professorships are just two examples of the enlarged channels of mobility. If that policy continues, as I think it will, then the upward shift it will create can come to mean a definite change in the orientation of the people who benefit from it; it can mean that successful blacks will begin to think like successful whites.

Blacks as the Most Recent Ethnic Group

Cox's clues regarding the importance of class have not generally been picked up and explored. By far, the greatest emphasis remains upon race alone as the defining dimension, with much less attention given to the effects of class. This bias increasingly will limit our understanding of what is happening. Recently, however, there have been some signs of class factors being given greater attention in the analysis of race and of racial inequalities. James O'Kane, for example, has expressed the view that most of what has happened historically and most of what is likely to occur in the future is more the result of class and less the result of racial differences.[34] He describes blacks as the most recent ethnic group in America, facing the same predicaments of the shift from rural to urban environments that once confronted immigrant ethnic groups. The fact of race is not denied, but, rather, it is placed within a class perspective.

However, what makes the case of blacks different from that of the immigrants is an economy that now has less room for unskilled occupations. "The rigidity of lower-class positioning and the increasing uncertainty of upward mobility thus create tensions in those individuals cut off from the prospects of improving their societal lot." And, O'Kane continues:

The problems and styles of life encountered in the lower-income Negro are not basically distinguishable from those of other ethnic groups, past or present. Certainly his family structure, his beliefs, and his values are different from those of the middle class. . . . Currently, the Negro comprises the most important ethnic group in the urban lower class. His problems and tragedies are those of preceding ethnic minorities, yet the profound economic changes in American society have greatly complicated his status and his potential for mobility.[35]

Class Versus Race

For O'Kane, racial considerations do not add very much to the understanding of these currents; in fact, they tend to becloud the central issue, which is the class differential. "The gap," he asserts, "exists between the classes, not the races; it is between the white and black middle class on the one hand, and the white and black lower class on the other. Skin color and the history of servitude do little to explain the present polarization of the classes."[36]

Yet, it is very probable that the class perspective has much less support than either of the other two perspectives that have been described. It has almost no constituency, once we subtract the great majority of whites who believe that race is primary and the great majority of blacks who, militantly or not, support racial separation. For the white segregationist, race is everything. For the white integrationist, race is almost as important, although admittedly for different reasons. As was explained in the discussion of black culture, race is given the highest priority—a fact reflected in the emphasis upon changing or amplifying the values ascribed to a black culture. Naturally, that emphasis depends upon which of the two alternative views of racial culture is chosen.

The cultural perspective, however, starts from the very questionable assumption that white and black populations are each rather homogeneous—in other words, that there is, at least, a unifying thread of black culture. In truth, though, black communities are as divided by class differences as are white communities. Indeed, there turns out to be a greater similarity between similar class groups across the races, than there is within each racial community. Whites who readily recognize the differences between lower-class and middle-class white persons, for example, somehow become blinded by race and forget that class differences play just as heavy a role for blacks. Of course, the insistence upon racial separatism by black militants has furthered acceptance of the concept by whites, just as it has been used to place race above class for its obvious political potential.

What evidence do we have to support the importance of class in this connection? Generally, very few studies have been conducted specifically to explore the view, even though such research should be given priority status. One of the best recent studies is that by Milton Rokeach and Seymour Parker.[37] A sample of about 1,400 adults was interviewed in 1968 by means of the Rokeach Value Survey, which consists of two sets of eighteen questions. With one set, called "terminal values," respondents were asked to rank such values as "a comfortable life," "freedom," "inner harmony," and "family security," in order of their relative importance. The second set, called "instrumental values," consisted of a ranking of such items as "ambition," "broadmindedness," "honesty," and "obedience." Responses were analyzed specifically to determine differences in the rankings between racial and class groups. Rokeach and Parker concluded that there were many differences between the way these values were ranked by low and high status groups. The former were "more religious, more conformist, less concerned with responsibility, more concerned with friendship than with love, and less concerned with competence and self-actualization."[38] With one exception, there were fewer value differences between black and white respondents than between respondents in different classes. The exception was the value given to "equality." Whites ranked it eleventh, and blacks ranked it second. Rokeach and

Parker concluded: "When status is held constant, or when poor whites and Negroes are compared with one another, most of the value differences previously found disappear or become minimal."[39]

From the black side of the race line, the militant gives relatively little attention to class in favor of race. The pursuit of class interests is unacceptable in large measure because it would dilute the singular primacy of race as a focus for identity, and loyalty, and, thereby, it would attenuate some of the political potential developed from racial identifications. The black bourgeoisie, for example, are explicitly villified by the militants because they make more of their class than of their racial position. In fact, the rise of the militant black ideology has introduced strong feelings of guilt among successful blacks who have not made their ties to the race explicit and evident. In any case, one consequence is clear: Class improvements through the opening of channels of mobility for blacks would seem to lead eventually to the growth of class consciousness at the expense of race consciousness. If that occurs, as it has among other ethnic groups in the U.S., then the power base of black-power groups will tend to shrink and erode, at least as long as that base is built entirely upon race.

Class and the Black Militant

Harold Cruse is exceptional among black intellectuals in his recognition of this developing dilemma for black militants.

Another important issue the Black Power theorists evade is the class problem among Negroes. When one talks bravely about developing political and economic black power one had best start clarifying which class is going to wield this power. . . . The [Black Power] theorists although they snipe at the black bourgeoisie, are themselves prey to bourgeois aspirations—major or minor. . . . However, the Black Power theorists are thrown into a reformist muddle involving class aspirations and economic power for the simple reason that they have no recognizable basis for economic power.[40]

Black successes, furthermore, must move the black leadership ever closer to a recognition of the growing importance of class for their cause. In effect, as long as most blacks were poor, then the black community was rather homogeneous as far as class was concerned. The gains of the last decade, though, have created class divisions, and class has begun to assume greater importance than ever before. In fact, James Laue has concluded that the earlier racial identifications that spurred the Movement have now been transformed.[41] What has been happening from 1960 to 1970, Laue judges, is that there have been a number of changes affecting the black middle class, including

vertical nationwide desegregation of public accommodations and facilities; registration of tens of thousands of black Deep South voters, and commensurate emergence of political power in some local situations; . . . black studies; Black

Power, black unity, black consciousness; significantly more jobs . . . ; hundreds of local projects for economic development, community development, self-determination; . . . consultation fees for rapping black.[42]

On the other hand, Laue concludes that "much less has changed for the grass roots ghetto" residents. The white-nonwhite disparities at the lowest class level are "staying the same or widening—in unemployment rates, life expectancy, infant and mother mortality, nonwhite median income as a percentage of white median income, etc." He concludes further that the issue no longer is so sharply a racial issue of integration as it was in 1960. Now, "[i]t is power . . . vs. no power. . . . This is the legacy of the 1960s[:] a politicized society in which the decision-making process at all levels is fair game for exposing and influencing." It *is* power that is central, and therefore, more is needed than just a strictly racial view, whether one is thinking politically or conceptually. The point of view that Oliver Cox described in 1948 finally became indispensable by 1970.

The class perspective introduces a necessary note of social reality into the consideration of racial inequality—a note that certainly is absent from the preceding cultural view and, to a lesser extent, from the income view as well. For above all, the class view includes the elementary recognition that the black's future depends upon successful political and economic integration, not necessarily racial, into American society. Indeed, this is what is at the crux of racial equality. Whether this is best achieved through black separatism at the beginning or through acceptance of existing institutional mechanisms is open to discussion as a matter of tactics, but, as the main objective, there should be no serious question about it.

Yet, black militant ideologists seem purposely to evade the class dimension in favor of the more romantic, but less realistic, nationalistic view. For example, Raymond S. Franklin can say: "We see that the ideology of Black Power, whatever its deficiencies, is irreversibly taking the Negro outside the market and outside the political framework which complements that market."[43] From his power base in the inner city, then, the black person can launch a "vast program—not for more welfare, make-work jobs, or integration—but for cultural, political, social and economic development."[44] This view is naive, for all its idealism. It simply overlooks the complexity of the struggles that must be raised by such an attempt, not the least of which as Cruse noted, is who in the black community is to control that power and set its direction. Is a growing black middle class going to endanger its position for the sake of racial goals? Why should they any more than the white middle class is ready to give up its privileges for the sake of achieving greater equality?

From the class perspective the problem is one of opening channels of mobility for blacks—channels that lead out of the lower class. Furthermore, the goal should be accomplished not simply through poverty programs but instead through the creation of effective and sustained opportunities. However, just as in the case of poverty, the stresses and strains upon the system come about when such channels are closed or blocked. The heightened aspirations among blacks are unmistakable, having been brought about by the gains made since 1954, and these must find expression or else American society is in for even greater violence and stress than we have had up until now.

From this perspective, then, the problem of racial inequality becomes one of committing blacks as a group to a permanently lower-class position by virtue of race alone. An inheritance of such inequality, thereby, becomes almost inevitable. The path to solution is not through a narrow income policy nor through the creation of intense black separatism, but through those means that will increase class mobility. As has been indicated, the real problem becomes whether or not the American class structure is flexible enough to permit such mobility and to reward the growing aspirations among blacks.

THE FUTURE OF RACIAL INEQUALITY

It is considerably harder to predict the future of racial inequality than to predict the future of poverty. The white poor, unlike the blacks, have no organization or leadership by which they can forcefully introduce their demands into the political arena. In addition, there is no basis for building identity among poor whites since there really is no unifying dimension other than class, and class consciousness is not easily developed. By contrast, blacks have organization, leadership, and a basis for identity, all of which have spawned a number of trends and countertrends both within black communities and in the relationships between blacks and whites. With the assassination of the Reverend Martin Luther King, American blacks lost the one leader who had been able to unify a large portion of blacks and also have access to the white power structure at the national level. Since that time, no one black leader has risen to command as wide a constituency.

The situation at present, then, is one of confusion and conflict between a number of potential leaders, all of them competing for the same basis of power support. Such competition, by itself, would make a prediction for the future quite problematic. Add on to this the growing animosity among the white working class and the lower-middle class toward blacks and the accuracy of prediction falls even more. What appears to be true at the present time is that an increasing dialectical spiral is developing. On the one hand, black demands are becoming ever more strident and insistent, fed by the competition for control between black leaders and black organizations. On the other hand, these demands and the violence associated with them have increased the intensity of the white backlash and the readiness of whites to take action in ways which tend to neutralize black demands.

Between these competing forces, the margin for maneuver and for a rationally directed improvement for blacks in America has narrowed.

For example, the sincere intentions of white reformers to spread the values and techniques of family planning have become interpreted by black militants as a form of racial genocide. The efforts at urban renewal become interpreted as attempts to split up black communities and, thus, to diffuse their political strength. From the other direction, attempts at setting black quotas for hiring in a number of skilled occupations raise the wrath of white working-class people who see their own hard-won gains as threatened and cheapened. The attempts at a better racial balance in the public schools enrage a good part of the white community, who resent and fight such interference. The general effect has been to make almost every program and every plan suspect, either by one side or the other. In this manner then, few, if any, actions turn out to be acceptable to the militants on both sides of the race line. Blacks will object to proposed programs because they do not go far enough or fast enough, while whites will object because those programs go too far or too fast. Under such circumstances, even a compromise solution can only succeed in alienating both groups.

The problems of racial inequality during the next decade, therefore, are likely to grow both in scope and intensity. It is hard to believe that the demands of black militants will be scaled down in the near future; after all, they need successes in much the same way that a professional politician needs votes. Nor is it likely that the intensity of the white backlash will abate in the light of such spiraling demands. Here, then, are two antithetical forces that, most likely, will continue to confront one another.

Moreover, I am not particularly optimistic about the balancing effect of the silent majorities, whether black or white. The changes in race relations since 1954, and for several more years to come, continue to narrow the ground on which the silent majorities can stand. For example, to a lower-class black with strong aspirations for upward mobility and a heightened level of expectations, the demands by black militant groups produce welcome signs of progress. Therefore, for a time at least, even the potential black bourgeoisie become partners with the militants. From the white side, the fears of privileged treatment for blacks—fears that are generated by the statements of segregationists—raise real reactions; increasingly, whites begin to leave the silent majority in order to join those leaders who give voice to their fears. The recognition of this fact of political life certainly has helped George Wallace's bid for national power.

Add on to these considerable trends the other problems of American society in this postindustrial era, and the problem of racial inequality is, indeed, even more confounded. The paths to social equality are no longer as simple as they once may have seemed, if only because political and economic institutions are themselves so complex. In the case of racial inequality, there is not only the problem of significantly altering long-held attitudes, but there is also the problem of making room in the structure for blacks to have equal class opportunities; in addition to the factor of race, therefore, there are the problems relating to class mobility—problems that were discussed in the preceding chapter. We have already seen how difficult the situation has become for whites, and the problems for blacks are even more difficult. At best, such problems require years of sincere effort if they are to be improved, but we are living in time when patience is a luxury.

5
The Future of Inequality

In the preceding pages, poverty and race have been described as problems of inequality in American society. Inequality, as stated at the outset, is as old as human societies and is not inherently a social problem. In every society, including our own, there exists a system of social stratification that separates, divides, and ranks the members of that society according to one or another set of criteria that generally are accepted as legitimate. In time, however, problems may arise because of changing attitudes and changing conditions. There may develop disagreements about the criteria; their legitimacy may be questioned, or the manner in which they are applied may become unacceptable. After all, even the presumed superiority of royalty, bolstered by religious supports, was not able to withstand the onslaught of new ideas that developed about individual freedom, dignity, and the natural law of human equality.

THE DILEMMA VERSUS THE DREAM

America may be more susceptible than most societies to the problems that can arise from social inequality, if only because it has been formally dedicated to the opposite proposition. Certainly it must be true that, if we had entered the modern era with the firm conviction that some people naturally were better than others instead of the view that everyone was naturally equal, we would have little basis for any problems arising from inequality. This is not to say that antiegalitarian beliefs have been absent, no matter what we have said about ourselves. Rather, one can suspect that many Americans have believed themselves to be superior to other Americans, having accepted the dictum of Don Alhambra del Bolero in *The Gondoliers* that "when everybody's somebody, then nobody's anybody." Still, we have given voice to the belief in equality even as we have practiced inequality. Myrdal was correct in identifying this national schizophrenia, but he was wrong in concluding that the condition necessarily led to an intolerable moral dilemma. Americans could and did live morally comfortable in spite of almost daily experiences with inequality because human sentiments are guided less by formal logic and more by a social logic, which permits the rearrangement and reinterpretation of social facts to fit one's needs.

Yet, if this condition has obtained for so long a time, why has inequality become so pressing a problem now? Certainly we have lacked neither poverty nor racial discrimination—discrimination that was manifestly much worse before 1954. Hunger, misery, slums, and racial violence are not recent American phenomena, and our relatively recent history included child labor, the feudal arrangements of company towns, black lynchings, and worse. By any comparison, in fact, the present is a marked improvement over the past—and precisely in regard to the above-mentioned social characteristics. Why, then, is the pressure for change so insistent at this particular point in time?

It surely must have been either almost purely accidental or as accidental as a major historical event can be. It was almost without any warning that the Supreme Court in 1954 unanimously decided to reverse the interpretation of the separate-but-equal doctrine and gave substance to a new drive for civil rights. Almost as dramatically, President Kennedy announced a war on poverty. Even such presumed accidents, however, need the proper social environment to nourish them. Americans, apparently, were ready for these significant events that reinterpreted the meaning of inequality.

Another reason is that the disparities between the poor and the affluent and between blacks and whites suddenly were brought into sharper focus. We began finally to see these disparities as being greater, sharper, more fixed, and more disappointing than ever before, even though we had thought that they were being improved. This occurred because American society had been changing. For instance, whereas once the majority of the black population lived in relatively rural isolation in a few states of the Deep South, the discrimination against them could be overlooked by most whites in much the same way as it was endured by most blacks. The urban concentrations of blacks by 1960 clearly projected racial differences as inescapable facts of life. Similarly, when wealth, comfort, and affluence were the privileges of a very few, then poverty was not exceptional. Today, by contrast, the proportions are no longer so lopsided, thanks to efficient production and advertisements for the better life. The evidences of poverty, thereby, stand out starkly because they are unexpected and because they apparently go so deep. After so many decades of overwhelming ourselves with the possibilities for economic advancement, we have made it virtually impossible for those who fail to rationalize their failures successfully.

Finally, the threshold of inequality that we can accept legitimately has been lowered as a result of change in our society. Partly, this is a function of increased social knowledge inasmuch as we understand that inequalities in voting, education, and employment lead to inequality everywhere else, no matter how motivated individuals actually may be to advance themselves. We can no longer take easy refuge in the rationalization that all poor people and all blacks deserve their inequality. Partly, we have come to recognize that equality of opportunities requires more than verbal support if it is to become real. Our traditional assumptions about such matters have been placed under closer scrutiny than we seem to have been ready to face in the past. As a result, we have been experiencing constant collisions between the traditional and the emerging patterns; we have been justly critical of some of the former but hardly ready to accept all of the latter.

This is neither the first, the last, nor the only contradiction we have to encounter within our institutions and within ourselves. We still speak of the values of free economic competition as if we were still a nation of small entrepreneurs; we still describe the political process as if it were a New England town meeting in which reasoned discussion and a rational vote determined public policies; and we still point to the ultimate power of the consumer as if the market still operated by the classical rules of supply and demand. The point is that all societies continually develop such contradictions between ideals and realities, between past and present. But the potential tensions created become especially severe when the values that are involved are vital ones or when there no longer seems to be any way to evade facing the contradictions we must face.

CUSHIONING THE CONTRADICTION

There are but a few alternatives by which to resolve these contradictions of collision. First, it is possible simply to dismiss them on the grounds that the current evidences of inequality are reasonable, necessary, and unavoidable. This amounts to saying that the institutions are still sound, that some inequality is natural, and that, in time, the contradictions will be canceled. After all, some people have to be at the bottom; not everybody can be somebody. Therefore, the reasoning that occurs all too frequently is that those at the bottom must have failed to take advantage of the opportunities open to them, and aside from trying to improve their condition for the sake of humanitarian reasons, we as a society owe them nothing further. For quite a long time, many Americans were willing to accept this view of inequality because it was easily legitimized by a reservoir of convenient wisdom: Poor people are lazy; blacks are naturally inferior; and anyone who really wants to get ahead can do it, et cetera. Rationalizations to justify the desired actions and beliefs were never really lacking. Although we have forced some changes in the rhetoric of convenient wisdom, a large number of Americans probably have never left this position, and more Americans appear to be attracted back to it.

An alternative view that can be used to cushion the contradiction is the belief that something is being done about inequalities. There is the recognition that inequalities did exist and that they continue to exist, but at the same time, it is coupled with the recognition that action is being taken to reduce some of those inequalities. After all, blacks have made observable advances in a variety of such areas as equal employment opportunities, open admissions to colleges, protected voting rights, improved housing, and financial assistance for black businesses. Nor have the poor been overlooked with regard to programs to improve the quality of their housing, their employment, and their training. Obviously, this is still a long way from full equality. But American institutions have been flexible, and changes have occurred. It is a view, for example, that has been attributed by a Canadian scholar, George Feaver, to a great many blacks who have "kept to the main road."

Though much maligned by white and black political nympholeptics who espouse facile solutions to racialism, they have set an example infinitely more to be admired. . . . [They have not been] deterred . . . in attempting to make a reality of their belief that the American democratic system, imperfect though it is, offers hopeful prospects for wide-ranging improvements . . . [S]teady (if hardly miraculous) progress *has* been made towards greater socioeconomic justice and expanded civil rights for the American Negro population.[1]

Finally, an additional alternative is that the contradiction can be accepted in full bloom as a serious indictment of the institutional processes of American society. Whatever gains have been made toward equality are not enough and only point up the inadequacy of the efforts. In short, either we move to redefine our traditional values about equality or else we move to change the institutional structure radically so as to bring it more into line with those values. In the case of racial inequality, this argument is central in the militant's rhetoric and his demands for greater control. For the poor, this argument is at the core of the attack upon the class system.

Among politicians, intellectuals, social scientists, and the public-at-large, adherents are to be found for each of the above-mentioned alternatives. Indeed, it is often the disagreement about the specific depth of the problem of inequality that produces the disagreement over the kind of program or action that needs to be developed. What is more to the point is that, over the several years of effort on behalf the poor and the blacks, many people have shifted their position among the various alternatives. For instance, I sense that a significant number of Americans have shifted from the second to the first alternative, in other words, from support for actions against inequality to simply leaving things alone. Having been made monotonously aware of poverty and racial discrimination, they have generally supported the government's efforts until quite recently. We have tried, they seem to contend, and further efforts will not yield any more results without, at the same time, endangering what has been accomplished by those who are neither poor nor black.

Probably, there is a smaller number of those who, having become disenchanted, have shifted from the second to the third alternative. Having become convinced from the evidence, or having inclined toward more serious changes from the start, these individuals now contend that our efforts to overcome inequalities are inadequate to the task and, therefore, that we now must move toward major changes of whatever form necessary.

Such complex changes in beliefs and attitudes are the result of individuals reacting to what is going on about them, and it is not to be implied that they are simply mechanical shifts. Indeed, there will continue to be changes throughout as new actions are taken and as individuals respond to them—a process which, in turn, will set the stage for subsequent actions. If nothing else, what we should have learned about the problems of inequality is that such problems are never static.

Granted that there are alternatives and that people change, what can be said about the future? Where is American society likely to go in the next several years?

THE TARNISHED FUTURE OF SOCIAL ENGINEERING AND OLD RHETORIC

One looks in vain for factually-based predictions that are objective, reasonable, and valid. Instead, one is almost immediately inundated either with social-engineering remedies or ideological rhetorics, both of which burst forth with a certainty of answers that belies the uncertainty of their underlying analysis. It is easy to illustrate the point by means of several examples that draw upon the literature of racial inequality. It is not claimed that the selection is representative of the total literature; the claim is only that the example is illustrative.

The studies sponsored by government agencies or commissions gravitate almost unerringly towards social-engineering solutions, in line with the sponsorship that wants suggestions for policy. The more cautious analysts may, and often do, surround their recommendations with the caveats of social research: the complexity of the problem, the need for more research, and the difficulties of providing feasible policy guidelines. Sooner or later, however, the analyst must nail down some specific recommendations because those are precisely what the sponsor wants, whether he intends to use them or not. One can sympathize with the difficulties inherent in such a situation and with the pressure to synthesize research findings so as to fit within the demands of the political process.

In a twenty-six page paper, Eli Ginzberg and Dale Hiestand touched on some aspects of black mobility in a report issued to the U.S. Commission on Civil Rights. It was a report that was meant to provide "guidelines for research on social and economic progress."[2] After stressing the "importance of improved data collection" and after making the inevitable point that "without additional understanding, policy will continue to be hit-or-miss," they concluded with a number of "strategic considerations" concerning education, housing, entrepreneurship, and employment. With regard to those factors, they set down the following suggestions for narrowing the gap of inequality between blacks and whites.[3]

- State and local governments should substantially increase their hiring and facilitate the promotion of qualified blacks.

- Government and business should continue to remain alert to the overt and covert discrimination that blocks the entrance and advancement of qualified blacks into many professions, and they should introduce and strengthen programs aimed at removing all such barriers.

- More educated blacks should enter strong graduate professional programs in science, engineering, business, journalism, and architecture; at the same time, more should seek to study medicine and law at prestigious schools.

These are excellent examples of what is meant by social engineering solutions. They are characterized by vagueness and coupled to the impossibility of putting them into practice. It is virtually impossible, in the case of the first directive, to produce any difference in the occupational mobility of a significant number of blacks, even if state and local governments could "substantially increase" such hiring. Now, as well as in 1968 when the report was written, they do not have anywhere near the funds necessary to carry out special employment in anything more than a token manner, and it can be assumed that the governmental units really would try to produce changes if they were to have the opportunity. One answer, of course, would be to fire substantial numbers of white employees and to replace them with blacks; that is a solution that some blacks have been advocating for some time. Such action might accomplish the desired result, but the result would be gained at a very high cost. One is left wondering, therefore, just how the recommendation was meant to be implemented.

The recommendation of stronger professional training for blacks is of a similar type, but it implies peculiar problems. No one denies the advantages of having blacks pursue postgraduate education so as to prepare them to compete more equitably with similarly educated whites for the better-paying occupations. Again, the matter of funds to support this educational push is left dangling. Qualified white students could be denied support, or additional funds could be acquired. Even so, the numbers involved are necessarily small, and one is left to wonder how long it would take for the advantages of this policy to filter down and to affect black communities significantly. Furthermore, what reason is there to believe that the individuals so assisted would identify with the aspirations of the black community?

Finally, the second recommendation illustrates additional vagueness. The phrase *remaining alert* specifies very little even though it conveys an impression of action. Further, even if one assumes that responsible governmental and business officials are deeply motivated by sincere intentions, they are not likely to know the many covert means of discrimination. There have been, and doubtless will continue to be, any number of reasons that can justify decisions involving blacks. Under such circumstances, it is hard to see how officials will be able to guard against discrimination.

Another example of the engineering solution is provided by Sar Levitan who has written frequently on the subject of poverty. In a reprint of his report on income-support programs, Levitan has set forth a number of priorities that could be geared toward the reduction of poverty. "Looking to the future," he concludes, "the most promising means of reducing poverty is to help the poor control the size of their families." And somewhat later he writes, "The first priority in the war on poverty should be given to dissemination of education about methods of birth control, and consistent with the religious beliefs of recipients, assistance should be made available to those who cannot afford private medical aid to plan parenthood. . . . "[4]

As long as the solution is kept simple, then its economic argument is logical: Smaller families will improve the economic position of the poor even without any increase in income. This is the same message that we have been drumming into the leaders of the developing nations for some time. Unfortunately, even neat economic solutions must encounter social and political realities in order to be effected. One can rightly wonder whether birth control can really be effective, particularly in view of the strident accusations by black militants that it is a white plot for black genocide. Such accusations cannot easily be disregarded, even though they have clear political strategies behind them. Further—omitting race—just what assurance is there that the eventual production of smaller families would lead to the desired results? At the very least, such a solution assumes that there will be no lowering of the amount of money disbursed to the poor; however, that cannot be assumed automatically in view of the financial pressures upon cities and states, particularly with regard to their welfare programs. Again, how will the existence of smaller families ease the core problem of inequality? Will it necessarily produce greater mobility for the poor even if the usual channels are still closed? Just how is the proposal meant to attack the problem of inequality? It is precisely at this point that engineering solutions go astray; they do so by assuming that, if only one or another symptom of the problem can be corrected, then the problem itself is on the way to being solved. It is the same logic that has caused many miles of expressways to be built in order to solve traffic congestion. What happens, in fact, is that the problem is changed, and sometimes the change is not even for the better.

The ideologically-inspired predictions and solutions, by contrast, are more complex than engineering solutions. The illustrations that have been selected are far from being transparent propaganda and, instead, are fully intended to be sincere statements of the situation. They are, in many instances, the products of scholarship in which the author appears to have reached his conclusions only after careful consideration of the facts. In any case, the purpose is to illustrate some ideologically-inspired predictions and solutions.

Until his death, Whitney Young was executive director of the National Urban League. His was a responsible position in a national organization, which doubtless had much to do with the point of view he expressed in his book, *Beyond Racism*. His tone is implicitly optimistic—that the great pressures of moral demands and decency are inescapable and that they must always lead in the desired direction. Of special relevance here is Young's statement in his concluding chapter.

Nothing will change until millions of white Americans, in the loneliness of their own consciences, face the truth about this country and begin to change their attitudes, from the inside out. The Open Society will be just one more treacherous dream until millions of black Americans organize themselves to seize the opportunities that are already there and win the opportunities that aren't.[5]

The moral uplift in Young's message does not find universal acceptance, especially among other black scholars who perceive quite different forces. Two black psychiatrists, William Grier and Price Cobbs, reached conclusions that are militant and demanding. According to their view, blacks in America are well past the state of passivity that earlier characterized their relationships with whites.

Not because blacks are so naturally warlike or rebellious, but because they are filled with such grief, such sorrow, such bitterness, and such hatred. . . . If existing oppressions and humiliating disenfranchisements are to be lifted, they will have to be lifted most speedily, or catastrophe will follow. For there are no more psychological tricks blacks can play upon themselves to make it possible to exist in dreadful circumstances. . . . Only a welling tide risen out of all those terrible years of grief, now a tidal wave of fury and rage, all black, black as night.[6]

The last two quotations, one by Young and one by Grier and Cobbs, are almost pure ideology stretched upon an intellectual frame. Both assume, for example, that there will be significant alterations in the attitudes of black persons because they have gained some recognition and a potential for expression. There is no doubt that attitudes among some blacks have changed and that those changed attitudes are a direct consequence of the improvements that have been made in the last decade. They exemplify a new sense of racial identity and a heightened sensitivity to the needs and rights of black people. Yet, the future direction of racial equality will depend very much upon the spread of these attitudes among large numbers of blacks, and it will depend upon the urgency with which they are held.

The fact that there are differences among black intellectuals and scholars as to the imminence of an apocalypse as described by Grier and Cobbs is evidence that the prophets are often speaking for themselves or for a small segment of those who think the same way. It is enlightening to compare the above quotation from Grier and Cobbs with the more measured conclusions of the black psychologist, Kenneth Clark, who is not at all convinced that the blacks really are going to go it alone.

White and Negro must fight together for the rights of human beings to make mistakes and to aspire to human goals. Negroes will not break out of the barriers of the ghetto unless whites transcend the barriers of their own minds, for the ghetto is to the Negro a reflection of the ghetto in which the white lives imprisoned. The poetic irony of race relations is that the rejected Negro must somehow also find the strength to free the privileged white.[7]

Clark, very much in the same manner as Whitney Young, sees the path toward racial equality as requiring some form of cooperation between whites and blacks, if only in the willingness of whites to "transcend the barriers of their own minds." Blacks simply cannot win the fight by themselves; it is not because they lack the ambition or dedication or motivation but rather because they are constrained by a society dominated by whites. Changes depend upon participation by both sides. The necessity for white participation in the search for racial equality is the dimension that the white sociologist, Lewis Killian,[8] identified as the barrier to radical changes. His pessimistic conclusion, quoted in the preceding chapter, was that the black revolution will not make it by fighting the white establishment.

As a final statement in the dialogue between white and black intellectuals—a dialogue that has been reconstructed above—one can cite the cautious conclusions of two white sociologists, Leonard Broom and Norval Glenn. They are two additional researchers who have studied the matter of cooperation between the races for the purpose of change.

Self-interest and, to an extent, humanitarian and ideological considerations will motivate some whites to crusade actively for Negro rights. Egalitarian values will prompt many more whites to limited support of Negro advancement that does not threaten their own interests. The underlying forces in the drama of American race relations will continue to be a complex of conflicting interests and conflicting values.[9]

The sum of these several quotations about the future of race relations and racial inequality is enough to document the impossibility of making valid and reliable predictions that are free from supposed ideological imperatives or social engineering mechanics. The situation is certainly not one of evil scholars serving as pure propagandists; after all, how many copies of their books were sold, how many were read, and who read them? The situation is that of complex variables continuing both to change initially and to force additional reverberating changes throughout the structural framework of the system.

The inequalities of poverty are as important as those of race—a fact exhibited by the varied array of literature on the subject. The subject attracts the social engineers and the ideologues, but the intensity level is lower than for race, if only because poor people do not write books. Because of the visible economic character of the problem, poverty attracts somewhat more engineering solutions than does the subject of race. Such solutions seek only to manipulate the symptoms of poverty, such as Levitan's proposal for family planning and birth control. Stylized in this manner, the "problem" of poverty seems to be instantly amenable to tampering, primarily economic, such as the setting of the discount rate by the Federal Reserve System. This approach often eventuates in a list of measures, such as the list proposed by Edward Banfield, who concludes his heavily ideological book with the suggestions below. He thinks the suggestions are feasible, but, in fact, they will be unacceptable to politicians, intellectuals, and other similar constituencies. Quoted are three of the twelve he has posited.

■   If it is feasible to do so . . . use fiscal policy to keep the general unemployment level below 3 percent. In any case, remove impediments to the employment of the unskilled, the unschooled, the young, Negroes, women, and others. . . .

■   Define poverty in terms of the nearly fixed standard of "hardship," rather than in terms of the elastic one of "relative deprivation," and bring all incomes above the poverty line.

■   Give intensive birth-control guidance to the incompetent poor.[10]

Banfield's suggestions come after more than two hundred pages of an argument that the problems of poverty and race are more nearly politically-inspired and intellectually-inspired problems rather than objective ones. The tone is reflected in the second proposal above, which asks for a redefinition of such problems in terms of an absolute standard rather than a relative one—a contention that runs throughout the book in one form or another. Novel as the idea might seem, it is impossible to accept because it falsely assumes that intellect and politics are not part of social reality. Certainly it is true that if we were to define poverty and racial inequality differently, as Banfield proposes, then they would be different problems, or perhaps they might even be made to disappear entirely. However, the fact that we define these problems as we do and that we take actions based upon this definition means that the definition is part of the reality and not simply an extraneous addition.

Indeed, as I have contended throughout, the perspective that one chooses has much to say about the nature of the problem that is identified and the kinds of solutions that can follow. Income, cultural, and class definitions of racial and economic inequalities are substantively different and lead to substantively different solutions. Still, a common thread that runs throughout these differences is the acceptance of the pursuit of equality as a primary American value. "A primary American value" is no empty phrase, no matter how cynical one may be about the success of that pursuit. After all, the value legitimates the recognition and the discussion of the problems of inequality; indeed, the value generates the fact that inequality is a social problem.

COMPONENTS OF CHANGE

The search for equality still continues to be a potent American goal, whether or not discernible progress is being made. It continues as the primary standard of appeal both for supporters and critics of any program or activity in government, political parties, and social groups. Often in the past the appeal has been more verbal than real, as instanced by the lofty expressions of support for equality in the midst of unmistakable and vicious prejudice and discrimination. Yet, the events of the past decade have forced some significant changes as regards the poor, the blacks, and the other minorities. For better or worse, we have agreed to scrutinize some of the institutional practices within American society and to change them where they obviously function to sustain and institutionalize inequalities. For example, the once rigid barriers against the full exercise of civil rights have been breached or lowered in a number of ways. So too, the denial to many citizens of their social rights to health, adequate housing, and education has been brought into public view, and some alterations have been instigated. In the process, Americans have learned something about their society and the way that it functions.

Above all, we have learned that the search for equality can still be considered necessary and that we cannot assume everything somehow will automatically correct itself. Things do not simply take care of themselves, no matter how much faith we may have that they do. Indeed, such blind faith has come into sharp question as we have become aware of the deficiencies of a system left to its own devices. Conscious, deliberate, and sustained intervention are demanded if we want the search for equality to continue. For instance, by allowing individuals to make their own choices as to where they want to live and where they can afford to live, we created the racial and economic segregation of our school systems. Segregation, in turn, fostered even more serious inequalities by freezing persons into their social positions in a way that we neither wanted nor anticipated. In order to correct the situation, it became necessary to intervene and to control the mix of students at great social, psychological, and economic costs. The effort has produced some unwelcome consequences and some violent reactions, but at least we were attempting to move in the right direction. Similar consequences have developed in other areas of social life as a conscious effort has been exerted to force needed changes. Yet, on balance, the effort to continue the search for equality should be more important than the undesirable and unexpected consequences of the moment. Important goals are never easy to achieve.

What about the future? What can we expect to happen next in the process of searching? No one really can predict the events of the next several years because we do not know the relative importance of the many factors that are involved, nor do we know the possible outcomes resulting from their mutual interaction. All we can be sure of is that so-called simple solutions turn out to be much more complex in practice as they generate their own effects.

To help avoid falling into the very trap that was illustrated previous-ly—the trap that is a direct result of following either the ideological or the social engineering solutions, it would be useful to specify three major components that generally will shape the future of inequality. The future probably falls somewhere between the dismal picture drawn by the revolutionary rhetoric and the simple expectations of the nuts-and-bolts solutions. In other words, as a society, we will neither change so radically that we become unrecognizable, nor will we solve everything by the simple plans that only tamper with the peripheral features of inequality.

The components can be identified as: (1) class, (2) metropolitan growth patterns, and (3) psychological perceptions.

Class

At the root of social inequality lies both the system of social stratifica-tion and the institutional processes that support it. Social stratification and its supporting processes represent the arena wherein we have long believed that self-correcting changes occur so as to keep the system open and, thereby, to provide everyone with relatively equal opportuni-ties. Instead, we have become conscious of the fact that this system does not operate so effectively in practice, and the result is that most people in all classes find themselves there through little fault of their own. Rich and poor alike have come to inherit their positions rather than to achieve them through their own efforts.

The nature of class dynamics is an important feature of future trends, and it constitutes a stumbling block upon which the social engineers as well as the ideologues falter. Ironically, they falter for different reasons. The social engineers run afoul because they do not consider the dynamics of the situation, and they turn instead to solutions that, at best, deal with symptoms rather than with causes. The ideologues fail because they read significance into events that simply are not there. The engineers who attempt to solve the problem of poverty, for example, believe that there must be some income policy that will be adequate to overcome inequalities, but they fail to see that such solutions do not greatly alter the relationships between classes. Income assistance to the poor does not serve to change their relative position; it only raises the ante.

The problem of the ideologues is somewhat different and a little more complex. Unlike the engineers, the ideologues rush to alter institutional structures and processes which they properly identify as requiring significant changes. Their error, though, is to believe their own rhetoric about the inevitability of revolutionary changes. They come to believe that everyone else must react as they do.

Some of the problem comes from the confusion about the meaning of "revolution." It has been used, according to Christopher Lasch, to mean "any profound social and political change"; to mean the changes that must come about "when existing structures lose their legitimacy and can no longer function without wholesale repression"; and to mean "the attempt . . . to seize state power on the part of political forces avowedly opposed not merely to the existing regime but to the existing social order as a whole."[11] Even if one can accept the most general definition of revolution in the first meaning above, it does not follow that America is moving unalterably in that direction. In spite of the revolutionary apocalypse foreseen by black nationalists, New Left students, and a variety of other intellectuals, there is still no basis for accepting the inevitability of their predictions. The error comes from believing that the contradictions and the repression seen by the revolutionaries are also seen by many others in the same way. It is a mistake that is illustrated by this quotation from the writings of Franz Schurmann.

The discussion over whether revolution in America is possible or not would have made sense a few decades ago. But today, America and other countries of the advanced capitalist world *are* in revolution. . . . [Revolutions] start with attacks on the moral-political order and the traditional hierarchy of class statuses. They succeed when the power structure, beset by its own irresolvable contradictions can no longer perform legitimately and effectively.[12]

If the Old Left is to be faulted for having been outdistanced by events or by having lost its ideology, then the New Left should be faulted for not understanding history or the significance of events, which they read not as facts but as their implacable vision. Changes have been occurring in the structure of classes and of class mobility and, as a result, we have been moving closer to an institutionalization of inequality in American society even though we still retain the traditional rhetoric of equality. However, no matter how cynical one might be about those efforts and their slowness, the society has been responding to some of the realities. If those responses expand and deepen—an effect brought about by the realization by many that contradictions do exist—then revolutionary change is not the only path open in the future. On the other hand, if those responses stagnate entirely, and if many other factors operate synergistically, then we may possibly move closer to a revolutionary situation. As Max Weber noted in one of his essays criticizing Marx, revolutions require an organized sense of community, not a mystical force of history. The point is that revolutionary actions are not the only and inevitable outcome of powerful social forces. For example, the growing disillusionment with the failures of poverty programs can still lead in either of the two directions just described, and it is highly premature to say which one it will be.

Black nationalists have run afoul of their own ideologies because they do not consider the class consequences of present events. As has been described earlier, the economic, political, and social gains made by segments of the black population are likely to mean a steady erosion of the nationalists' constituency, and the result would probably be the loss of the most talented segment of that constituency. The successful gains for blacks will transform an increasingly greater portion of the lower class into a working class or a middle class with commitments to the system that made the gains possible.

Even the most optimistic view at this time is that America appears to be moving toward the creation of more and more class antagonisms and class contradictions. However, the force and direction of those trends is not preordained, nor is it fully predictable. Obviously, there is still latitude for a number of other factors to intervene and to shape those trends. No class is, as yet, in the clutch of history, and rational changes are still possible. Still, it must be in the context of the class system that the problem of inequality will have to be resolved, not at the periphery of the matrix of symptoms.

Metropolitan Growth

The demographic trends related to the growing division between the central cities and the suburbs have significance for the future of inequality because the American population has been segregating itself. Geographic segregation, in other words, is leading to important social changes as the population divides into sectors and each sector grows ignorant of the others.

To its credit, the National Advisory Commission on Civil Disorders had identified this trend in 1968 and had warned of the consequences of a continued separation consisting of blacks and poor in the central cities and the affluent and whites seeking refuge in the suburbs. These sharp disparities have continued, and very little is being done to correct them. Our traditional policies about private property and local politics have remained virtually unaltered from what they were decades ago, so that we continue to encourage suburban expansion as we turn away from the central cities and their problems. Any effective action for change, thereby, is frustrated by our insistence upon retaining traditional governmental boundaries that no longer are adapted to existing functional boundaries.

This kind of demographic segregation is now new; every American city, throughout this century and even earlier, was similarly divided into class and racial neighborhoods. The difference now is the effective geographic spread that serves to isolate class and race groups from each other. The central city ghetto in this decade, as seen from a car that is traveling at the rate of 50 m.p.h., is not the same view one gets by either driving more slowly or walking through the streets. The neighborhoods do not have the same appearance they would have had 50 years ago. Physical separation has come to mean social and psychological separation as well. Hence, the conditions of life for the poor of both races in the inner city remain known only to the inhabitants and to a handful of outsiders such as the police, firemen, TV reporters, and social workers whose duties bring them into the ghetto.

The effect of this condition is to distort seriously the impressions that affluent Americans have about the costs of inequality and discrimination. At best, the general impressions impute to today's poor an image based upon the affluents' experiences of a generation or more ago but covered over with a patina of romantic nostalgia. If this is the silent majority, then many of them are silent because of ignorance.

One does not have to be a naive environmental determinist to accept the likelihood that these ecological conditions have a great deal to do with one's perception of reality. To the middle-class suburbanite, as well as to the poverty family in a central city slum, the world comes to be defined realistically by surroundings. The intimate and sensory experiences of the individual must affect his conceptual ideas, and, because of that fact, we are likely to be in the process of creating many different images of reality depending upon residential location.

There are political dimensions to demographic segregation—a reality the mayors of large cities are discovering almost daily. As the suburbs have come to be defined as the locales of the good life, so the central cities have become identified as the locales of the life of inequality. The central cities have been forced to assume the role of institution keeper for the seamy side of American society. We have saddled them with almost all of the ills of urban society but without any of the advantages. Physically segregated, we have insisted that central cities play this most undesirable role so as to avoid any strong confrontation with our contradictory values. Even violent riots can be contained within the central cities without causing most suburban dwellers a single minute of difficulty.

This situation represents a growing danger to the future shape of American society. Geopolitically, for instance, we are in effect turning over more and more of our central cities to black monopolies, since blacks comprise growing majorities of more and more cities. Herein are to be found the new causes of inequality. Further, there is the likelihood that class antagonisms will continue to sharpen in the future as a result of this kind of urban ecology, although one is less inclined to accept the view that such antagonisms will necessarily become organized and, thereby, will become the basis for open class warfare. Hence, it is difficult to agree with Franz Schurmann's assessment:

As the poor live in the cities and the middle class in the suburbs, we can say that the class war in the United States is taking the form of an antagonistic relationship between city and suburb. The suburban middle class has a stake in the economy. The urban poor are excluded from it.[13]

The class antagonisms between suburb and city certainly are real enough, but we ought not to assume that nothing will be done to change them or that such antagonisms will automatically gravitate into class actions. Neither assumption is certain.

Yet, the search for equality must incorporate significant changes in the pattern of geographic segregation that we have permitted to develop. The creation of change means deliberate institutional intervention. As has been implied previously, some of our most treasured beliefs about the rights of private property, the freedom of entrepreneurial real estate developers, and the immutability of governmental boundaries need to be scrutinized if we believe that the value of equality is worth it. The engineering solutions here, as in the case of poverty—scattered-site public housing for the few, school busing, or the like—simply are inadequate. We very likely have created more animosity and resistance by such programs than we would have by more meaningful interventions. In any case, we no longer can afford to overlook these metropolitan growth patterns if we intend doing something lasting about inequality.

Psychological Perceptions

The last component of change depends upon individuals themselves and their perceptions of the events around them as well as their reactions to those events. Lash and backlash are generated by such perceptions, and no plan or prediction about the future can afford to overlook their role in shaping events.

Black intellectuals and black politicians have succeeded in giving voice and substance to the demands for racial equality. For the first time in American history the black perspective has become known better, and it has become known by more people than ever before. Behind the angry demands and the militant rhetoric there lies a perspective that is more subtle and more complex than simply the grab for power. It is what Harold Cruse has called the black's "ethnic conception of reality";[14] the black perceives that he is a member of a group in which he wishes to place himself rather than one into which he is forced by the racial perceptions of whites. In order to survive, the black must avoid isolating himself and thereby pursuing what Cruse calls "The Great American Ideal of Individualism," but instead, he must become ethnically identified because America "is in reality a nation dominated by the social power of groups, classes, in-groups, and cliques—both ethnic and religious." Whites, who up to a point are willing to extend material improvements to blacks, generally miss the close relationship between the demands for improvements and the orientation from which they are made. The result has been continued tensions and misunderstanding as that relationship slowly becomes manifest. On the side of the blacks, the error has been to assume that all whites are equally guilty and that they are all incapable of understanding.

Just how resistant white persons will be to accepting the blacks' orientation depends very much on what they perceive as the consequences. If it produces something such as a black version of Protestants, Catholics, Jews, Italians, Poles, or Irish, then that is one thing. If, on the other hand, it produces a tightly knit and cohesive social grouping that threatens everyone else, then the white reaction is likely to be more repressive and sharp. The first situation rather than the second represents the more likely outcome because the gains made by blacks are likely to fractionate them into smaller groupings. Regardless of what quite a few black intellectuals believe, the division of black communities into classes is the most likely outcome of the present period. A residue of black ethnicity may remain, bolstered by a developing sense of history and tradition, but its force will diminish. If these assumptions are correct, then the racial component of inequality may well decrease in importance in the years ahead.

CHANGE—THE ULTIMATUM OF NECESSITY

The changes and reactions related to economic inequality are less clear, simply because the poor are so heterogeneous a population. There is no ethnic identity here upon which to build group cohesion. In fact, there is no dimension, other than poverty itself, that could serve to unite the poor into anything even resembling an effective social group—a condition that is only further compounded by the differences among the poor (leaving race aside) with respect to age, physical ability or disability, and the like. Earlier, as now, the poor have had to depend upon outsiders—intellectuals, politicians, demagogues, and reformers—to identify their plight and to make their case. This condition makes their demands no less real or no less important, but it leaves the poor at the mercy of either humanitarian or base impulses of others. Unfortunately, there is little ground for optimism about the willingness of Americans to continue even a skirmish on poverty, let alone a war. Only the recognition that poverty is a problem of inequality that strikes deep at the roots of American institutions can yield significant changes in the situation of the poor.

Unfortunately, one rapidly becomes anesthetized by the crisis rhetoric which has been so overused in recent years. All difficulties become problems, and all problems become crises; all alterations become changes, and all changes become revolutions. Inevitably under these conditions, we lose the sense of priority by which we can intelligently allocate our energies and resources to a hierarchy of social demands. Confusion is the only result of assigning as equally important, traffic congestion, air pollution, drug addiction, prison reform, and inequality. At the very minimum, therefore, we must organize our priorities upon some rational basis instead of frantically chasing each new "problem" as it attracts our attention. So far, the situation has been analogous to an attempt to keep up with the latest style of automobile as soon as it is produced in Detroit.

Of highest rank in any reordered list must stand the future of inequality. Here, indeed, is a matter that is literally of vital concern for the future shape of American society. If we give up the search for equality or are misled into expending our resources for all other types of problems, then we might indeed have to prepare for the apocalypse that is being predicted for us.

Reference Notes

Chapter One

1. Leslie A. Fiedler, *Being Busted* (New York: Stein and Day Publishers, 1969).
2. Orlando Fals Borda, "Marginality and Revolution in Latin America, 1809–1969," *Studies in Comparative International Development,* 6 (1970–71), 63–89.
3. Michael Harrington, *The Other America: Poverty in the United States* (Baltimore: Penguin Books, Inc., 1966).
4. William Ryan, *Blaming the Victim* (New York: Pantheon Books, Inc., 1971).
5. W. J. Cash, *The Mind of the South* (New York: Anchor Books, Doubleday & Company, Inc., 1954), p. 305.
6. Alexis de Tocqueville, *Democracy in America,* translated by George Lawrence and edited by J. P. Mayer (New York: Anchor Books, Doubleday & Company, Inc., 1969), p. 9.
7. *Ibid.,* p. 54.
8. Seymour Martin Lipset, *The First New Nation* (New York: Basic Books, Inc., Publishers, 1963), p. 341 and p. 343.
9. S. M. Miller, review article of *The Great Society's Poor Law* by Sar A. Levitan, in *The Annals of the American Academy of Political and Social Science,* 385 (September 1969): 175.
10. T. V. Smith, *The American Philosophy of Equality* (Chicago: University of Chicago Press, 1927), p. 252.
11. I have tried to document the role of the white middle class in the South as far as the move toward racial equality is concerned. See Leonard Reissman, "Social Development and the American South," *Journal of Social Issues,* 22 (January 1966): 101–16.

Chapter Two

1. *Report of the National Advisory Commission on Civil Disorders* (Washington, D.C.: U.S. Government Printing Office, 1968), pp. 3–15.
2. Hugh Davis Graham and Ted Robert Gurr, *Violence in America* (New York: Bantam Books, Inc., 1969).
3. Gunnar Myrdal, *An American Dilemma,* Twentieth Anniversary Edition (New York: Harper & Row, Publishers, 1962), p. lxxi.
4. R. H. Tawney, *Equality* (New York: Harcourt Brace Jovanovich, Inc., 1931), pp. 48–49.
5. Edward C. Banfield, *The Unheavenly City* (Boston: Little, Brown and Co., 1970).
6. Robert Nisbet, "The Urban Crisis Revisited," *The Intercollegiate Review* (Fall 1970), p. 7.

7. W. J. Cash, *The Mind of the South* (New York: Anchor Books, Doubleday and Company, Inc., 1954), p. 22.

8. Quoted in T. V. Smith, *The American Philosophy of Equality* (Chicago: University of Chicago Press, 1927), pp. 14–15.

9. Smith, *op. cit.,* pp. 32–33.

10. Donald R. Matthews and James W. Prothro, *Negroes and the New Southern Politics* (New York: Harcourt Brace Jovanovich, Inc., 1966), p. 15.

11. *Ibid.,* p. 481.

12. Alexis de Tocqueville, *Democracy in America,* translated by George Lawrence and edited by J. P. Mayer (New York: Doubleday and Company, Inc., Anchor Books, 1969), p. 56.

13. Reported in the *New York Times* (March 25, 1970), p. 27.

14. Melvin M. Tumin, "Some Principles of Stratification," *American Sociological Review,* 18 (August 1953): 389.

15. Robin M. Williams, Jr., *American Society,* Third Edition (New York: Alfred A. Knopf, Inc., 1970), pp. 472–79.

16. *Ibid.,* p. 477.

17. *Ibid.,* p. 591.

18. S. M. Miller, "Comparative Social Mobility," *Current Sociology,* 9, No. 1 (1960): 4.

19. Peter M. Blau and Otis D. Duncan, *The American Occupational Structure* (New York: John Wiley & Sons, Inc., 1967), pp. 423–39.

20. Leonard Reissman, "Readiness to Succeed," *Urban Affairs Quarterly,* 4 (March 1969): 379–95.

21. Frank Parkin, "Class Stratification in Socialist Societies," *British Journal of Sociology,* 20 (December 1969): 368.

22. Seymour Martin Lipset and Reinhard Bendix, *Social Mobility In Industrial Society* (Berkeley: University of California Press, 1959), pp. 284–85.

23. *Ibid.,* pp. 286–87.

Chapter Three

1. E. M. Schreiber and G. T. Nygreen, "Subjective Social Class in America: 1945–68," *Social Forces,* 48 (March 1970): 348–56.

2. Warren C. Haggstrom, "Can the Poor Transform the World?" in Irwin Deutscher and Elizabeth J. Thompson, eds., *Among the People: Encounters With the Poor* (New York: Basic Books, Inc., Publishers, 1968), pp. 67–68.

3. Bureau of the Census, "Socioeconomic Trends in Poverty Areas, 1960 to 1968," *Current Population Reports,* Series P–60, No. 67 (Washington, D.C.: U.S. Government Printing Office, December 30, 1969).

4. Bureau of the Census, "24 Million Americans—Poverty in the United States: 1969," *Current Population Reports,* Series P–60, No. 76 (Washington, D.C.: U.S. Government Printing Office, 1970), p. 1.

5. Bureau of the Census, "Poverty in the United States: 1959–1968," *Current Population Reports,* Series P–60, No. 68 (Washington, D.C.: U.S. Government Printing Office, 1969), p. 1.

6. Bureau of the Census, "The Extent of Poverty in the United States, 1959 to 1966," *Current Population Reports,* Series P–60, No. 54 (Washington, D.C.: U.S. Government Printing Office, 1968), p. 2.

7. Edward C. Banfield, *The Unheavenly City* (Boston: Little, Brown and Co., 1970), p. 124.

8. The President's Commission on Income Maintenance Programs, *Background Papers* (Washington, D.C.: U.S. Government Printing Office, n.d.), p. 12.

9. S. M. Miller and Pamela A. Roby, Chapter 2, "Poverty as Income Deficiency: Three Approaches," in *The Future of Inequality* (New York: Basic Books, Inc., Publishers, 1970).

10. *Ibid.,* p. 34.

11. *Ibid.,* pp. 35–37.

12. President's Commission on Income Maintenance Programs, *op. cit.,* p. 12.

13. Oscar Lewis, quoted in Charles A. Valentine, *Culture and Poverty* (Chicago: University of Chicago Press, 1968), p. 129.

14. Valentine, *op. cit.,* p. 141.

15. Lee Rainwater, "The Problem of Lower Class Culture," *Journal of Social Issues,* 26 (Spring 1970): 146.

16. Valentine, *op. cit.,* p. 144.

17. Peter H. Rossi and Zahava D. Blum, "Social Stratification and Poverty" (multilith). A paper presented at the annual meetings of the Sociological Research Association (August 1967), p. 107.

18. William Ryan, *Blaming the Victim* (New York: Pantheon Books, Inc., 1971), pp. 134–35.

19. Valentine, *op. cit.,* p. 142.

20. Miller and Roby, *The Future of Inequality, op. cit.,* p. 3.

21. The Report of the President's Commission on Income Maintenance Programs, *Poverty Amid Plenty: The American Paradox* (Washington, D.C.: U.S. Government Printing Office, 1969), p. 14.

22. For a concise description of the negative income tax, the guaranteed income and other income-support programs, see the essays in Herman P. Miller, (ed.), *Poverty: American Style* (Belmont, Calif.: Wadsworth Publishing Co., 1966), Chapter 8.

23. A. L. Kroeber, *Anthropology* (New York: Harcourt Brace Jovanovich, Inc., 1948), pp. 274–76.

24. S. M. Miller and Frank Riessman, *Social Class and Social Policy* (New York: Basic Books, Inc., Publishers, 1968), p. 58.

25. Arthur Pearl, "The Poverty of Psychology—An Indictment," in Vernon L. Allen, ed., *Psychological Factors in Poverty* (Chicago: Markham Publishing Co., 1970), the quotations taken from pp. 348–63.

26. Valentine, *op. cit.,* p. 15.

27. Miller and Riessman, *op. cit.,* pp. 58–59.

28. Lewis A. Coser, "Unanticipated Conservative Consequences of Liberal Theorizing," *Social Problems,* 16 (Winter 1969): 270–71.

29. David Matza, "The Disreputable Poor," in Neil J. Smelser and Seymour Martin Lipset, eds., *Social Structure and Mobility in Economic Development* (Chicago: Aldine Atherton, Inc., Publishing Co., 1966), pp. 311–12. Along the same lines see Miller and Riessman, *op. cit.,* pp. 52–56, who distinguish between (1) the undeserving poor who "are not interested in being self-supporting," (2) the self-defeating poor who are incompetent, and (3) the victimized poor who are the "results of the ineffective or pernicious working of society, long-time discrimination," and the like.

30. Miller and Riessman, *op. cit.,* pp. 38–42.

31. The point is well made by S. M. Miller and Pamela A. Roby, "Poverty:

Changing Social Stratification," in Daniel P. Moynihan, ed., *On Understanding Poverty* (New York: Basic Books, Inc., Publishers, 1969), p. 64.

32. Joan H. Rytina, William H. Form, and John Pease, "Income and Stratification Ideology: Beliefs About the American Opportunity Structure," *American Journal of Sociology,* 75 (January 1970): 703–16.

33. Leonard Reissman, "Readiness to Succeed: Mobility Aspirations and Modernism Among the Poor," *Urban Affairs Quarterly* 4 (March 1969): 379–95.

34. Rossi and Blum, *op. cit.,* p. 53.

35. Rytina, *et al., op. cit.,* p. 713.

36. *Ibid.*

37. Joe R. Feagin, "American Attitudes Toward Poverty and Anti-Poverty Programs" (mimeo.), A Final Report on NIMH Research Grant (May 1971).

38. *Ibid.,* p. 26, Table 9.

39. Rytina, *et al., op. cit.,* p. 715.

40. Miller and Roby, "Poverty: Changing Social Stratification," *op. cit.,* p. 79. See also, S. M. Miller, *et al.,* "Poverty, Inequality and Conflict," *Annals of the American Academy of Political and Social Science,* 373 (September 1967): 16–52, but especially 51–52.

Chapter Four

1. Bureau of the Census, "The Social and Economic Status of Negroes in the United States, 1970," *Current Population Reports,* Series P–23, No. 38 (Washington, D.C.: U.S. Government Printing Office, 1971), pp. 35, 48, 60, 77, 98, 102, and 114.

2. I. A. Newby, *Challenge to the Court: Social Scientists and the Defense of Segregation, 1954–1966* (Baton Rouge: Louisiana State University Press, 1967), p. 9.

3. Reported in Newby, *op. cit.,* pp. 216–17.

4. The citations of authority in what became the famous "Footnote Eleven," in the Court's decision included some of these works: Kenneth B. Clark, *Effects of Prejudice and Discrimination on Personality Development;* Max Deutscher and Isidor Chein, "The Psychological Effects of Enforced Segregation: A Survey of Social Science Opinion"; E. Franklin Frazier, *The Negro in the United States;* and Gunnar Myrdal, *An American Dilemma.* All quoted in Newby, *op. cit.,* p. 5.

5. Kenneth N. Vines, "Courts and Political Change in the South," *Journal of Social Issues,* 22 (January 1966): 71.

6. Bureau of the Census, "The Social and Economic Status of Negroes in the United States, 1970," *op. cit.,* p. 83. In 1964, 51 percent of all black college students were in predominately black colleges, but in 1970 this proportion had dropped sharply to 28 percent.

7. *Report of the National Advisory Commission on Civil Disorders* (Washington, D.C.: U.S. Government Printing Office, 1968). p. 1.

8. *Ibid.,* p. 7.

9. St. Clair Drake, "Urban Violence and American Social Movement," in *Urban Riots,* Robert H. Connery, ed. (New York: Vintage Books, Random House, Inc., 1969), p. 26.

10. M. Elaine Burgess, *Negro Leadership in a Southern City* (Chapel Hill: University of North Carolina Press, 1962). See also, Daniel C. Thompson, *The Negro Leadership Class* (Englewood Cliffs, N.J.: Prentice-Hall, Inc., 1963).

11. Eli Ginzberg, ed., *The Negro Challenge to the Business Community* (New York: McGraw-Hill Book Company, 1964), p. 85.

12. Sumner M. Rosen, "Reflections on Economic Development in the Ghetto," *The Urban Review*, 4 (May 1970): 15.

13. *Ibid.*

14. *Ibid.,* p. 18.

15. U.S. Department of Labor, *The Negro Family* (Washington, D.C.: U.S. Government Printing Office, 1965), p. 5.

16. Bureau of the Census, "Fertility Indicators: 1970," *Current Population Reports,* Series P–23, No. 36 (Washington, D.C.: U.S. Government Printing Office, 1971), p. 42.

17. *The Negro Family, op. cit.,* p. 29.

18. *Ibid.*

19. Lee Rainwater and William L. Yancey eds., *The Moynihan Report and the Politics of Controversy* (Cambridge: The M.I.T. Press, 1967).

20. Elizabeth Herzog, "Is There a 'Breakdown' of the Negro Family?" in Rainwater and Yancey, *op. cit.,* pp. 352–53.

21. Lewis A. Coser, "Unanticipated Conservative Consequences of Liberal Theorizing," *Social Problems,* 16 (Winter 1969): 270.

22. Frank Riessman, "In Defense of the Negro Family," in Rainwater and Yancey, *op. cit.,* p. 475.

23. Herbert H. Hyman and John Shelton Reed, " 'Black Matriarchy' Reconsidered," *Public Opinion Quarterly,* 33 (Fall 1969): 346–54.

24. *Ibid.,* p. 354.

25. Harold Cruse, *The Crisis of the Negro Intellectual* (New York: William Morrow & Co., Inc., 1967), pp. 6–10.

26. *Ibid.,* p. 8.

27. A term taken from Leo Kuper, "Structural Discontinuities in an African Town," in *The City in Modern Africa,* Horace Miner, ed. (New York: Praeger, 1967), pp. 135–38. Kuper defines "parallel structures" as a "basic structural separation of the racial groups" with effective control under the politically dominant group.

28. *Ibid.,* p. 137.

29. Quoted in Colin Legum, "The Black Establishment," *New Society* (April 18, 1968), p. 556.

30. *Ibid.*

31. Lewis M. Killian, *The Impossible Revolution* (New York: Random House, Inc., 1968), pp. 172–76.

32. G. Franklin Edwards quoted in Legum, *op. cit.,* p. 558.

33. Oliver C. Cox, *Caste, Class, and Race* (New York: Doubleday & Company, Inc., 1948).

34. James M. O'Kane, "Ethnic Mobility and the Lower-Income Negro: A Socio-Historical Perspective," *Social Problems,* 16 (Winter 1969): 302–11.

35. *Ibid.,* p. 310.

36. *Ibid.*

37. Milton Rokeach and Seymour Parker, "Values as Social Indicators of Poverty and Race Relations in America," *Annals of the American Academy of Political and Social Science,* 368 (March 1970): 97–111.

38. *Ibid.*, p. 110.

39. *Ibid.*

40. Cruse, *op. cit.*, p. 560.

41. James H. Laue, "The Movement: Discovering Where It's At and How to Get It," *Urban and Social Change Review,* 3 (Spring 1970): 6–11.

42. *Ibid.*, p. 8.

43. Raymond S. Franklin, "The Political Economy of Black Power," *Social Problems,* 16 (Winter 1969): 299.

44. *Ibid.*, p. 301.

Chapter Five

1. George Feaver, "The Panther's Road to Suicide: A Black Tragedy," *Encounter,* 36 (May 1971): 42.

2. Eli Ginzberg and Dale L. Hiestand, *Mobility in the Negro Community,* U.S. Commission on Civil Rights, Clearing House Publication No. 11 (Washington, D.C.: U.S. Government Printing Office, June 1968).

3. *Ibid.*, p. 23.

4. Sar A. Levitan, "Alternative Income Support Programs," in Herman P. Miller, ed., *Poverty American Style* (Belmont, California: Wadsworth Publishing Co., 1966), p. 282.

5. Whitney M. Young, Jr., *Beyond Racism: Building an Open Society* (New York: McGraw-Hill Book Company, 1969), p. 205.

6. William H. Grier and Price M. Cobbs, *Black Rage* (New York: Bantam Books, Inc., 1968).

7. Kenneth B. Clark, *Dark Ghetto* (New York: Torchbooks, Harper & Row, Publishers, 1965), p. 240.

8. Lewis M. Killian, *The Impossible Revolution?* (New York: Random House, Inc., 1968).

9. Leonard Broom and Norval Glenn, *Transformation of the Negro American* (New York: Colophon Books, Harper & Row, Publishers, 1965), p. 191.

10. Edward C. Banfield, *The Unheavenly City* (Boston: Little, Brown and Company, 1968), pp. 245–46.

11. Christopher Lasch, "Epilogue," in Roderick Aya and Norman Miller, eds., *The New American Revolution* (New York: The Free Press, 1971), p. 318.

12. Franz Schurmann, "System, Contradictions, and Revolution in America," in Aya and Miller, *op. cit.*, pp. 75–76.

13. *Ibid.*, p. 60.

14. Harold Cruse, *The Crisis of the Negro Intellectual* (New York: William Morrow & Co., Inc., 1967), p. 6.

Index